# Walking in Victory

## Through the Power of God's Word and His Spirit

PRODUCED BY PALM TREE PUBLICATIONS
A DIVISION OF PALM TREE PRODUCTIONS
KELLER, TEXAS 76244
PRINTED IN THE U.S.A.

www.palmtreeproductions.net

---

Unless otherwise indicated, all Scripture quotations are taken from *The Amplified Bible* (AMP), *The Amplified Bible, Old Testament*, copyright © 1965, 1987 by The Zondervan Corporation. *The Amplified New Testament*, copyright © 1954, 1958, 1987 by The Lockman Foundation. Used by permission.

Scripture quotations marked "NIV" are taken from the *Holy Bible, New International Version*® (NIV®), Copyright © 1973, 1978, 1984 by International Bible Society. Used by permission of Zondervan Publishing House. All rights reserved.

Scripture quotations marked "NKJV" are taken from the *New King James Version*, Copyright © 1982 by Thomas Nelson, Inc. Used by permission. All rights reserved.

Cover Design & Interior Layout by: Wendy K. Walters | www.palmtreeproductions.net
Author's Photograph by: Tim Randall | www.timrandall.com

# Walking in *Victory*

## Through the Power of God's Word and His Spirit

© 1996—2009 Gaye Moss.

All Rights Reserved. This book or any portion of this book may not be reproduced in any form without first obtaining written permission from the author.

---

ISBN: 978-0-9822237-6-5

---

Contact the author or order additional copies at:

www.GayeMoss.com

# DEDICATION

To my husband, Pete—

    my daughter, Mindy—

        and my son, Michael—

I dedicate *Walking in Victory* to you. I am so grateful for your loving support and patience as I have pressed through to a life of walking in victory.

To my mother, Mildred Howard—

Thank you for being an amazing example of God's love, grace, and faithfulness.

To my friend and prayer partner, Nancy—

Thank you for always believing in me and giving me encouragement to publish this study.

To my loving and faithful friends—

Thank you for your continued and ongoing love and support.

# Endorsements

Gaye Moss is a deep well of wisdom and grace. Reading her study gave me the opportunity to drink from her well. Each lesson has a clear outline, applicable scriptures and a powerful sample prayer that makes it easy to incorporate the information and make it your own. Her vulnerability and personal examples are not only engaging but also allow you to learn through her spiritual trials and triumphs.

Gaye's study is rich with divine insight and her writing style makes it easy for the reader to apply the lessons and achieve a whole new level of obedience, joy and peace. She has a gift for taking profound spiritual truths and communicating them in simple lessons that have deep, life-changing impact. I have the incredible honor of being personally under the mentorship of this remarkable teacher. I am excited that this opportunity is extended to each of her readers through the publication of this study.

**RYANE NICHOLS MOATES**
*Euless, Texas*
*www.MoatesArt.biz*

Several years ago, I was privately struggling in many areas of my life. I knew and admired other believers who were experiencing great victory in their marriages, families and finances, but it all seemed so out of reach for me. Most of the time, I felt like a fake. As a brand-new stay-at-home mom, I joined a Bible study called Walking In Victory, taught by Gaye Moss.

From the first lesson on the first day, little sparks of hope began to ignite in my heart. It was as if the secret to victorious living in Christ was being unzipped before me! As Gaye presented scripture after scripture, the promises of the Word of God came alive to me in a way that I had never experienced. The revelation that God holds victory in store for all of His children, who choose to believe Him and His Word, changed the course of my life. And I have never been the same.

If you are a mature believer, Walking In Victory will take you to new, deeper levels of faith. If you are young in your faith, this study will cultivate the soil of your heart, stirring up and fertilizing your faith so that it can grow and flourish.

**TAMMY ADAMS**

# Endorsements

*North Richland Hills, Texas*

I had the privilege of going through this study the first time 13 years ago. Walking In Victory includes so much scripture that it inspired me to dig deeper and study the Word in a way I had not done before this study. It gave me a hunger for more of the Word, and it gave me knowledge as to how to apply it to my life. I have gone through the study three times now, and it is fresh and new every time! I have carried it around in my purse for the last three years because I love using it as a reference and guide. I have really enjoyed serving in women's ministry with Gaye. She is an accomplished and gifted teacher of the Word.

**AMY NORMAND**
*Hurst, Texas*

I first met Gaye Moss through a women's group at Gateway Church. I will never forget the words that she said to me upon our very first meeting: "I feel like I love you already!" I believe that she is truly the most loving person I know, and she lavishes her love upon all who are blessed and honored to sit under her teaching. Gaye is a remarkable communicator and has been teacher, mentor and friend to countless women through the years. She is spoken of with the highest regard and honor. For many, she has been the hands, feet and voice of Jesus.

Gaye Moss' Walking In Victory study springs forth from a deep well of intimacy with the Lover of her soul. Her motivation comes from a desire to love and know Him and His ways in the fullest and to share what she has learned. She has experienced, first hand, the power of God's Word and His Spirit that transforms lives and leads us into victory. This study will challenge you to look beyond your circumstances and reach for higher places of revelation and experiences in the Lord, while providing practical insight on how to get there.

**LISA WATSON**
*Bedford, Texas*

# Endorsements

*I am so excited for all who will have the opportunity to go through this life-changing study. It has been pivotal in my spiritual life. When I first met Gaye, I was a service-oriented Southern Baptist girl who loved Jesus with everything I had, but I was lacking a life of walking in victory. Then, I was led to this study. I've gone through the study twice, and I've purchased it for my adult sons. I highly recommend it to everyone!*

**JULIE AVARY**
*Colleyville, Texas*

*Working through the Walking In Victory study helped me see how my life really can be a victorious one. It showed me how to rely on God's Word and Spirit to guide me and fill me. Gaye Moss does a beautiful job of exciting her reader to want to know the Lord on a deeper level. She shares practical truths for how to call upon the power of scripture and the Holy Spirit to bring freedom and victory into your life. It is a study not to be missed.*

**CHRISTINA LAWLESS**
*Flower Mound, Texas*

*Walking In Victory is a "how-to" manual for the overcoming Christian life. It couples the power of the Spirit with biblical truths to ignite the true freedom every believer desires. It partners with Jesus' words when He spoke of the phenomenal power of believers to bind the darkness and loose the kingdom. This study specifically targets how to defeat fear and self-diminishment, through the sword of the Spirit, which is the Word of God, and ultimately, gain life and live it abundantly!*

**REBECCA BERRY**
*Euless, Texas*

# Endorsements

*Do you ever wonder how anyone, even believers, could feel like a winner while going through life's most difficult situations? Walking In Victory can help shift the way you view your circumstances through kingdom perspective. This Bible study is essential for everyone in any stage of life who wants to increase his or her faith in the Lord. Gaye Moss is a gifted teacher and communicator, and she is an incredibly graceful woman of God. I have been personally impacted by her teaching and counsel, and now through Walking in Victory, you, too, will discover the keys of tremendous revelatory insights to live every day victoriously through Gaye's personal journey and powerful testimony of God's amazing grace and loving touch. Walking In Victory is written in a transparent style that is rooted in the Word of God.*

**ELENA GLASSMAN**
Lewisville, Texas

*I had the privilege to sit under Gaye's teaching in the study Walking In Victory, and it truly changed me from within. Gaye is a gifted teacher with a heart for women and their true freedom in Christ. She really has the ability to relate and connect with her audience in sincere humility. Her heartfelt compassion is worn on her sleeve, and the revelation and teaching in this study is as good as I have seen!*

**KERRIE OLES**
Living Divine Ministries
Carrolton, Texas

*Gaye Moss has a wonderful, unique way of teaching. I have learned so much about the Holy Spirit and the authority we have as believers. Whether you are new in your faith or you have walked with the Lord for many years, you will be strengthened, refreshed, and blessed as you go through Walking In Victory.*

**PEGGY DICKERMAN**
Bedford, Texas

*Walking In Victory is an excellent study that I have used and recommended to disciple and mentor women and men of all ages. As you move chapter by chapter through the study, you will receive revelation through the scriptural truths that are shared that will powerfully strengthen and encourage your faith. You cannot help but be transformed by the power of Jesus' Word and His Spirit as you take time to dig deep into this wonderful study. Be ready to be blessed abundantly!*

**NANCY CAVE**
*Keller, Texas*

*Every once in a while a book comes along that can change your life. This study is one of them. In its pages you will find a powerful message that needs to be heard. Open the pages of this study and begin a life-changing journey!*

**TEENA GOBLE**
*Prayer Care Ministries*
*Colleyville, Texas*

*Gaye Moss' Walking in Victory study is the most well rounded Bible Study I have ever read. I found myself looking forward to digging deep into each lesson. I was always built-up and encouraged. It was literally a lifeline during an extremely difficult season of my life. Gaye's study left me with the resounding Truth that God is good, He is Love, and He has thoroughly equipped each of us to live a life of victory.*

**JOYA WOTILA**
*Bedford, Texas*

# Table of Contents

NOTE TO LEADERS AND GROUP MEMBERS — 11

INTRODUCTION — 13

### Lesson One
EXPERIENCING GOD'S ABUNDANT LIFE — 15

### Lesson Two
EXPERIENCING TRUE PROSPERITY IN GOD — 29

### Lesson Three
THE POWER OF LOVE — 45

### Lesson Four
THE POWER OF OBEDIENCE — 59

### Lesson Five
GOD WILL GIVE YOU STRENGTH AND POWER — 75

### Lesson Six
EXPERIENCING GOD'S ABUNDANT JOY — 87

### Lesson Seven
EXPERIENCING GOD'S WONDERFUL PEACE — 101

### Lesson Eight
GOD WILL GIVE YOU WISDOM — 115

### Lesson Nine
LIVING IN VICTORIOUS FAITH — 129

### Lesson Ten
RECOGNIZING WHO YOU ARE IN CHRIST — 147

ENDNOTES — 165

# NOTE TO LEADERS AND GROUP MEMBERS

These lessons are written to be interactive. It will be very helpful for group members to spend time praying and thinking through the answers to the questions prior to the group each week. As you pray through the Scriptures and questions, God will give amazing insight and revelation.

**Leaders and Group Members** Ask the Holy Spirit to direct the group discussion each week. Pray that you will be sensitive to His leadership when answering questions. It is always exciting to watch as the Holy Spirit directs and leads.

**Leaders** There will be weeks that the group discussion goes so well that it is difficult to complete the lesson. If time permits in your schedule, you may want to start the next week at the point where you ended the lesson the preceding week. It will be helpful, if possible, to schedule more than 10 weeks for the study so that you do not need to rush through the answers to the questions. Lessons 9 and 10 are extra long, and they may require more than a week to cover them adequately.

In addition to group studies, this study has been used as a personal devotional. I have received awesome feedback from those who have used it as a devotional. It has also been used in one-on-one mentoring with great success.

The truths in this study have radically changed my life. Every time I review these powerful truths I receive deeper revelation and insight. I pray that God will reveal amazing and life-changing things to you as you go through these lessons. Regardless of the stage of your Christian journey, I know you will be blessed.

*Gaye Moss*

# INTRODUCTION

It is very exciting when we discover that God is for us, and He has a wonderful plan for our lives. There are many people who live their entire lives without an understanding that God is good, and He desires the highest and best for each individual life.

God has given us many tools to assist us in living a victorious life. It is His sincere desire to see us fulfill the destiny that He has planned for us. When we receive the precious gift of eternal life through Jesus Christ, we can know with certainty that all things are possible with God, and He holds victory in store for us. God longs to see us walking in victory every day.

Even through the most difficult circumstances of our lives, we can walk in victory. When we are resting and trusting in the truths and promises of God's Word, and we are depending on the comfort, strength, and power of the Holy Spirit, we can maintain a life of victory no mater how difficult the situations we face.

In times of pain, confusion, struggle, and doubt, there is a place we can run to for God's wisdom and His answers to our questions. Through the presence of the Holy Spirit and the promises of the Word of God, we will find refuge and comfort.

When life seems dark and hopeless, God's Word and His Spirit will bring light and hope. When there is confusion all around us, God's

Word and His comforting presence will bring us peace. When there seems to be only sadness, God will restore our joy. Day-by-day and moment-by-moment we can depend on the Word of God and the Spirit of God to lead us and guide us into victory.

God's Word is full of promises and instructions that enable us to enjoy abundant, Spirit-filled, transformed lives. God has given us His powerful promises and instructions to bless us. As we follow His precepts, and we listen closely to His counsel, we will be strengthened and empowered. Through faithfulness and obedience to the insight we receive, we will experience more and more of God's amazing life imparted to us. Jesus came that we might have full, complete, and abundant life (John 10:10).

The study of God's Word, with the help and the revelation of the Holy Spirit, is the most exciting journey we can imagine. As we go through this study, we are going to examine amazing biblical principles concerning the power of the Word of God to bring true freedom to our lives. As we diligently commit ourselves to God's powerful Word and the awesome leadership of the Holy Spirit, our lives will be wonderfully changed.

There is nothing that compares to the Spirit-filled life that Jesus imparts to us. There is nothing that can fill our lives and comfort us like Jesus can. He will lift us out of depression, discouragement, hopelessness, despair, and so much more when we choose to place our trust in His life-changing Word and the power of His Spirit.

# EXPERIENCING GOD'S ABUNDANT LIFE

*"The thief comes only in order to steal and kill and destroy. I came that they may have and enjoy life, and have it in abundance (to the full, till it overflows)."*
*John 10:10*

**Lesson Focus:** Through God's Word and His Spirit we receive outstanding revelation and insight that will enable us to walk in the abundant life that Jesus came to give us—life that overflows with His goodness, grace, mercy, and love.

**Introduction:** It is Jesus' sincere desire that we enjoy our life. He longs for us to experience abundant life. He wants our lives to overflow with the good things of His kingdom. The more we renew our minds to the truths and promises of His Word, and the more we walk in obedience to His instructions, yielding to the leadership of the Holy Spirit, the more we will experience true victory in Christ.

We are given a wonderful picture in 2 Corinthians 9:8 of God's abundance. In this verse Paul says, *"God is able to make all grace (every favor and earthly blessing) come to you in abundance, so that you may always and under all circumstances and whatever the need be self-sufficient [possessing enough to require no aid or support and furnished in abundance for every good work and charitable donation]."*

When we receive Jesus as our Savior and Lord, we receive His amazing grace. Jesus told us in Luke 4:18-19 that He was anointed to bring good news, freedom, and release for the oppressed. He came *"to proclaim the year of the Lord's favor"* (NIV). All who place their faith and trust in Jesus step into His favor and grace.

God has awesome things in store for each of us regardless of what is taking place in the world around us. He has marvelous blessings for us regardless of our enemies. He will take our enemies' plans to harm us and use them for our good (Genesis 50:20). He will give us wisdom (James 1:5), and He will show us the right path to take (Proverbs 3:5-6). He works all things together for our good (Romans 8:28). His love is limitless and it never fails (1 Corinthians 13:8).

In this lesson, we will examine valuable scriptural principles and foundational truths that will launch us into a life that overflows with the good things of the kingdom of God. These biblical principles will enable us to achieve the joy-filled life that God desires for each of us. He tells us in Jeremiah 29:11, *"For I know the plans I have for you, declares the Lord, plans to prosper you and not to harm you, plans to give you hope and a future"* (NIV). God has great things planned for our lives. Living a life that is led by the Spirit of God and the Word of God is very exciting and rewarding.

# SIX VALUABLE STEPS TO EXPERIENCING ABUNDANT LIFE IN GOD

## 1. Surrender Yourself Completely to God.

To live the full and abundant life that Jesus desires for us it is absolutely essential to dedicate and surrender ourselves completely to God. Paul makes this sincere and earnest appeal in Romans 12:1:

> *I appeal to you therefore, brethren, and beg of you in view of [all] the mercies of God, to make a decisive dedication of your bodies [presenting all your members and faculties] as a living sacrifice, holy (devoted, consecrated) and well pleasing to God, which is your reasonable (rational, intelligent) service and spiritual worship.*

 According to Romans 12:1, what is the reasonable and intelligent thing for us to do in our service and worship of God?

 Would you make a fresh commitment today to surrender yourself completely to God?

Yielding our lives totally and completely to God is the reasonable and sane thing for us to do. God knows what is best for each of us. He has a perfect plan for our lives, and when we yield to His will and His plan, we will succeed in life.

## 2. Be Transformed by the Renewing of Your Mind.

In Romans 12:2, we find another extremely important step to living an abundant life. In this verse we are told:

> *Do not be conformed to this world (this age), [fashioned after and adapted to its external, superficial customs], but be transformed (changed) by the [entire] renewal of your mind [by its new ideals and its new attitude], so that you may prove [for yourselves] what is the good and acceptable and perfect will of God, even the thing which is good and acceptable and perfect [in His sight for you].*

**Question:** What instructions are we given in Romans 12:2?

**Question:** According to this verse, why is it so valuable for us to renew our minds?

A renewed mind is the avenue to knowing God's perfect will for our lives. Jesus will show us the plan and the way to live victoriously as we yield to Him. He is the Source of our faith, and He is the Finisher of our faith (Hebrews 12:2). As our thoughts line up with His thoughts, we will know the right path to take in every situation because we will be following the One who knows the way to genuine victory.

The Holy Spirit authored the Scriptures, and He will help us bring our thoughts into agreement with the mind of Christ (2 Corinthians 10:5). As our thoughts line up with God's thoughts, we will have all the wisdom and direction we need to live successful lives.

When I was in my late twenties, I experienced first hand the transforming work of the Word of God. At that time, I was invited to a Bible Study where I met some remarkable ladies who gave me valuable insight into the power of God's Word to impart life and health (Proverbs 4:20-22). They stressed over and over the importance of the Word of God combined with yielding to the Spirit of God.

A number of years later, when I found myself in a desperate place emotionally, God led me to spend concentrated time reading, studying, and meditating in the Scriptures. As I stayed in the Word, I made heart commitments to walk in obedience to God's instructions. I was determined to walk in the fullness of all that God desired for me. The longer I stayed in the Word, the more freedom and victory I experienced. Through the power of the Word and the Spirit, I was able to break free from the bondage that was causing the emotional pain.

## 3. Hold Fast to Truth.

We renew our minds with Truth from God's Word. Therefore, it is extremely important for us to understand scriptural truths. Jesus gives us clear instructions regarding the importance of biblical Truth in John 8:31-32:

> *So Jesus said to those Jews who had believed in Him, if you abide in My word [hold fast to My teachings*

*and live in accordance with them], you are truly my disciples.*

*And you will know the Truth and the Truth will set you free.*

**Question:** According to John 8:31-32, what makes us true disciples?

**Question:** According to these verses, where do we find the Truth that sets us free?

**Question:** According to the following verses, how do the truths of God's Word bless our lives?

- Psalm 119:9—

- Psalm 119:24—

- Psalm 119:41-42—

- Psalm 119:45—

- Psalm 119:138—

- Psalm 119:165—

uestion: How have Scriptural truths brought freedom to your life?

There are many things that are true in our world that do not bring freedom, but the truths we find in God's Word will set us free. The Truths from God's Word are powerful. As we hold fast to Jesus' teachings and live in accordance with them, we will walk in genuine victory.

**THERE ARE MANY THINGS THAT ARE TRUE IN OUR WORLD THAT DO NOT BRING FREEDOM, BUT THE TRUTHS WE FIND IN GOD'S WORD WILL SET US FREE.**

Every battle we face with the enemy of our souls is a battle for Truth. Satan was disarmed and defeated at the cross (Colossians 2:15). He has no power or authority over a believer other than lies and deception. Every believer has been given power and authority over all the power of the enemy (Luke 10:19). Lies are Satan's only means of holding us in bondage. When we are anxious, fearful, discouraged or depressed, we need to ask God to show us the lies that are causing these emotions. Then we need to ask God to reveal Truth to us from His Word that will contradict the lies.

When we agree with our enemy, we become fearful and depressed. When we agree with God, we will walk in faith and courage. Our enemy loses his hold on us when we agree with the Truth of God's Word.

While standing at my kitchen sink one morning, feeling very disheartened and discouraged, I asked the Lord, "Why am I feeling so discouraged?" I heard Him say, "What have you been thinking?" I said, "I have been thinking that the situation that I am in is impossible." Then I heard Him say, "What does my Word say?" At that moment I realized that I had believed a lie, and I said, "Your Word says, 'Nothing is impossible with God' (Luke 1:37)." When I saw the Truth, all the discouragement lifted.

We are set free when Truth is revealed. Scripture tells us that God is for us (Romans 8:31). God is on our side, and He is completely trustworthy. Nothing can separate us from the love of God, and therefore, there is no reason to be discouraged, depressed or fearful. We have an all-powerful God who is completely faithful. He loves us and He will make a way for us as we place our trust in Him. The more we renew our minds to the wonderful truths found in the Word, the more we will be released from the chains that bind us.

## 4. Be Cleansed by the Washing of the Word.

There is an awesome cleansing and purifying work that takes place in our lives through the Word of God. As we spend time in the Scriptures, God's Word works as a cleansing fountain that removes impurities from our lives. As the Truth flows into our lives, impurities surface and they are washed away. Paul gives us insight into this process in the book of Ephesians. While giving instruction to husbands to love their wives, Paul reveals the love of Christ for His church and the power of His Word to cleanse. He writes in Ephesians 5:25-27:

> *Husbands, love your wives, as Christ loved the church and gave Himself up for her, so that He might sanctify her, having cleansed her by the washing of water with the Word.*
>
> *That He might present the church to Himself in glorious splendor, without spot or wrinkle or any such things [that she might be holy and faultless].*

 According to this passage, how important is the Word of God if we desire freedom for our lives?

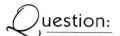 According to these verses, what can we trust the Truth of God's Word to do for us?

Through the instructions and the truths that I discovered while pressing into the Word of God for emotional healing, I began to walk in new levels of freedom. Little-by-little, God's Word changed my old thought patterns. Day-by-day and week-by-week, my mind was renewed, and the wrong patterns of thinking were cleansed and replaced with God's Word. With each new discovery, I experienced greater measures of God's peace and joy.

I had fallen into an emotional trap, and I desperately needed to be released. I was very vulnerable, but God was watching over me the entire time. He was so gracious and patient with me. He waited for me to cry out for help. When I did, He faithfully led me to freedom.

God's cleansing and liberating work in my life continues to this day. It is an ongoing process for which I am very grateful. We live in a fallen world, and it is important for us to stay in the cleansing fountain of God's Word. The blood of Jesus washed away all our sin and shame at the cross. His Word cleanses and renews our minds so that we can fully enjoy the cleansing work of the cross.

## 5. Keep God's Word in the Center of Your Heart.

Vast riches of Truth are imparted to us as we meditate in God's Word and receive revelation from His Spirit. There are amazing treasures of wisdom to be received through sitting in God's presence. Keeping God's Word in the center of our hearts is essential to living a victorious life. It is our life source. We read in Proverbs 4:20-22:

> *My son, attend to my words; consent and submit to my sayings.*
>
> *Let them not depart from your sight; keep them in the center of your heart.*
>
> *For they are life to those who find them, healing and health to all their flesh.*

 What are we instructed to do in this passage, and what will be the outcome if we follow these instructions?

 How has attending and submitting to God's Word made a difference in your life?

During the time frame that I was seeking emotional healing, every time I opened my Bible I would say, "Lord, I am taking my medicine." I spent two months reading through the entire Bible specifically for healing of my emotions. As I read, I made decisions to accept and follow the instructions and counsel I received.

By the end of the two months, I began to experience amazing freedom. I had no idea that kind of freedom existed. It was as if

I had been released from chains that had been holding me in bondage for years. Until I received the comfort and liberty that the Word and Spirit brought to me, I did not know how genuinely bound I was. I had been bound for so long that it seemed normal. As the chains that were binding me broke off, I began to experience indescribable joy and peace.

## 6. Make God's Word Your Delight.

We find confirmation in Psalm 119 regarding the power and importance of the life-giving source of God's Word. The psalmist tells us:

> *This is my comfort and consolation in my affliction; that Your Word has revived me and given me life (Psalm 119:50).*

> *Unless Your law had been my delight, I would have perished in my affliction. I will never forget Your precepts, [how can I?] for it is by them You have quickened me (granted me life) (Psalm 119:92-93).*

> *The entrance and unfolding of Your words give light; their unfolding gives understanding (discernment and comprehension) to the simple (Psalm 119:130).*

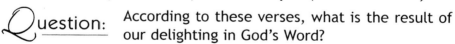 According to these verses, what is the result of our delighting in God's Word?

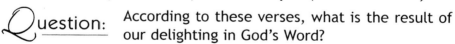 How has God's Word brought comfort, consolation, and life to you?

The following statement by Andrew Murray communicates so well the importance of delighting in the Word of God. He writes:

> *True life is found only in God. But that life cannot be imparted to us unless set before us in some shape in which we know and apprehend it. It is in the Word of God that the Invisible Divine life takes shape and brings itself within our reach, and becomes communicable. The life, the thoughts, the sentiments, and the power of God are embodied in His words. And it is only through His Word that the life of God can really enter into us. His Word is the seed of the Heavenly life.*[1]

Have you ever thought of God's Word as being the seed of Heavenly life? When we plant God's Word in our hearts, staying sensitive to the voice of the Spirit and remaining diligent in prayer, we will see amazing results. We want to remain focused and vigilant in this process, guarding and protecting our hearts from any lies or assignments of the enemy.

> **WE CAN ALWAYS REST AND TRUST IN THE FAITHFULNESS OF GOD, EVEN IN THE MOST DIFFICULT CIRCUMSTANCES.**

As we learn to rest in God's promises for our lives, we will know and experience His incredible peace and comfort. We can always rest and trust in the faithfulness of God, even in the most difficult of circumstances. Through the power of God's Word, we will learn to soar in our spiritual life. Through biblical Truth, we will rise above the attempts of our enemy to defeat and destroy us.

## Lesson Application:

Take some time to ask God to show you any lies that you have believed from the past, along with any lies that you presently believe. Then ask Him to show you Truth from His Word that will answer and cancel out those lies. Ask God to lead you to Scripture that will reveal the Truth you need for the situations in which you are involved at this point in time. Take those scriptural truths, precepts, and promises and begin to meditate on them until you have them firmly planted in your heart.

*"For with God nothing is ever impossible and no Word from God shall be without power or impossible of fulfillment."* Luke 1:37

*Dear Lord,*

*Thank You for the powerful truths found in Your Word. Thank You for the amazing counsel and instruction You give to me through Your Word and Your Spirit. Open the eyes of my heart to receive valuable insight and understanding each time I read and study Your Word. Thank You for enabling me to walk in Your Truth every day. I know that nothing is ever impossible with You, and no Word from You will ever be without power or impossible of fulfillment (Luke 1:37). Help me to walk in every promise and precept of Your powerful Word.*

*In Jesus' precious name,*
*Amen*

*Lesson Two*

# EXPERIENCING TRUE PROSPERITY IN GOD

*"If you will listen diligently to the voice of the Lord your God, being watchful to do all His commandments... the Lord shall make you have a surplus of prosperity..."*
*Deuteronomy 28:1, 11*

**Lesson Focus:** As we spend time in God's Word and His presence, listening to His voice and obeying His counsel, we will walk in true prosperity.

**Introduction:** True prosperity in God involves far more than earthly possessions. It is so much more than simply having material goods and earthly wealth. To walk in true prosperity is to walk in God's wonderful love and joy and peace, along with all the amazing aspects of the fruit of the Spirit. It includes walking in the gifts and anointing of the Spirit of God. It knows the wonder and fullness of God's goodness, mercy and kindness.

God longs for us to live a full and blessed life. He longs for us to know the fullness of His love and grace and all that He has provided for us. As we saw in lesson one, Jesus came that we might have abundant life. It is His will to see us prosper in every area of life.

It is our Heavenly Father's sincere desire to see us blessed. Just as earthly parents desire to see their children blessed, God desires the same for His children. His desire is higher and deeper than we can imagine. When we come into the family of God, we enter into the kingdom realm where there are limitless possibilities. God longs to take us to new heights and new depths in our understanding of His love and grace. The blessings of God are immeasurable for those who are rooted and established in His love (Ephesians 3:16-21).

> **WHEN WE COME INTO THE FAMILY OF GOD, WE ENTER INTO THE KINGDOM REALM WHERE THERE ARE LIMITLESS POSSIBILITIES.**

God made a covenant with the children of Israel while they were in the wilderness. Through their covenant, we have a wonderful picture of God's desire to bless His people. He promised the children of Israel cities and houses they did not build, wells they did not dig, and vineyards and olive groves they did not plant (Deuteronomy 6:10-11). It was God's will and desire for the world to see and know His goodness through the blessings He bestowed on His chosen people.

The children of Israel were not able to remain faithful to the covenant God made with them. However, it was prophesied that a Savior would come, the Messiah, and He would bring the fullness of God's blessings to those who would place their trust in Him. He would be the source of a new covenant that would be far superior to the old covenant that was sealed by the blood of goats and calves (Hebrews 9:12).

The new covenant would be sealed with the precious blood of Jesus (Hebrews 9:14-15). This was accomplished at the cross. All who have committed their lives to Jesus have the royal privilege of walking in His amazing grace and blessings. Jesus redeemed us to walk in the fullness of God's grace and love. He paid our debt in full, and He has blessed us *"in the heavenly realms with every spiritual blessing in Christ"* (Ephesians 1:3).

As we abide in Jesus, He gives us power and ability to accomplish everything that He has called us to accomplish for His glory. He enables us to enter into the realm of the Spirit where there is endless potential and promise.

# FIVE VALUABLE KEYS TO WALKING IN DIVINE PROSPERITY

### 1. Abide in Jesus and Keep His Word in Your Heart.

As we continually abide in Jesus, He will enable us to bear much fruit (John 15:5). It is important for us to remember that it is only through abiding in Jesus that we bear fruit. Apart from Him we cannot accomplish anything of real value. Jesus told His disciples in John 15:7-8:

> *If you live in Me [abide vitally united to Me] and My words remain in you and continue to live in your hearts, ask whatever you will, and it shall be done for you.*
>
> *When you bear (produce) much fruit, My Father is honored and glorified, and you show and prove yourselves to be true followers of Mine.*

 According to John 15:7-8, why is abiding in Jesus and keeping His words in our hearts so important?

***Question:*** According to these verses, why is it important for us to have God's Word living in our hearts when we pray?

***Question:*** As you consider Jesus' words of instruction in John 15:7-8, what is true success?

I often ask Jesus to give me a verse of Scripture as I begin my day. An encouraging verse always ministers wonderful life to me at any point in the day. God's Word is alive (Hebrews 4:12), and it imparts strength and life to us. It is better than vitamins. We are told in Isaiah 55:11 that the Word of God does not return void. It always brings good things to us. When we focus on the Word, our faith grows. That is why Jesus tells us that we will see answered prayer when we abide in His Word. A very discouraging day can be turned completely around with one encouraging verse of Scripture.

Living and abiding vitally united to Jesus and His Word enables us to know His will. When we know His will, we know how to respond in faith, and we know how to pray successfully. As we respond in faith, we bring honor and glory to our Heavenly Father.

## 2. Yield to the Holy Spirit.

Jesus sent us an amazing Counselor to help us in our commitment to abide in Him. When we are full of questions and uncertain as to what to do, we can draw on the wisdom and counsel of the Holy Spirit. The Holy Spirit will bring our thoughts into agreement with the Word of God. He is always faithful to remind us of Scripture verses that speak to our need. We find valuable instructions in John 6:63 regarding the importance of the Holy Spirit. Jesus tells us:

> *It is the Spirit Who gives life [He is the Life-giver]; the flesh conveys no benefit whatever [there is no profit in it]. The words (truths) that I have been speaking to you are spirit and life.*

In John 14:26 Jesus says:

> *But the Comforter (Counselor, Helper, Intercessor, Advocate, Strengthener, Standby), the Holy Spirit Whom the Father will send in My name [in My place to represent Me and act on My behalf]. He will teach you all things. And He will cause you to recall (will remind you of, bring to your remembrance) everything I have told you.*

 According to these Scripture verses, why is the help and counsel of the Holy Spirit important?

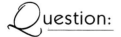 What did Jesus tell us about His words in John 6:63?

The importance of the Holy Spirit in receiving life from the Word became very clear to me at a time when I was given an assignment at my church to read the book of Romans. During that period of my life, I was diligently seeking to know God on a deeper level. While reading through Romans, I remember thinking that it was confusing. At times it seemed contradictory to me.

Several days after reading through Romans, I became convicted that I needed to let go of some resentment that I was harboring in my heart. I knew that I needed to be obedient to God's Word regarding forgiveness, so I prayed a simple prayer asking for help. That night after my children were in bed and it was quiet in the house, I realized that all of the resentment that I had been feeling earlier was gone. I was very excited. I began praising God saying, "Lord, You are wonderful. You are amazing. Thank You for hearing and answering my prayer."

While I was offering my praise to God, I had an experience that felt like liquid love was being poured from the top of my head to the soles of my feet. I did not know that a love like that existed. It was extraordinary! The Lord spoke some very comforting words to me, and He began to give me insight into another situation in my life where I needed to forgive. It was as if all resentment was washed from my heart that night.

I made an appointment the next day to talk with my pastor. He told me that I had encountered the Holy Spirit. He said that when I began to praise God, He poured out the comforting presence of the Holy Spirit. I had experienced God's help through my prayer. As I praised Him, I experienced the wonderful comfort of the Holy Spirit. My pastor told me to read chapters 14, 15, and 16 of the gospel of John. In these chapters, Jesus tells His disciples that He is sending the Holy Spirit to be their Counselor, Comforter and Helper.

An amazing thing happened after the tremendous outpouring of God's love. I read through Romans again, and a whole new revelation and understanding of the book opened up to me. It no longer seemed confusing or contradictory. The Holy Spirit gave me understanding that I did not have a few days earlier. From that time forward, I began to experience the Holy Spirit as my Counselor, Helper, and Friend.

## 3. Meditate on the Word of God.

God gave some very powerful instructions regarding meditating on His Word to Joshua. In Joshua 1:7-8, He told him:

> *Be strong and very courageous, that you may do according to all the law which Moses My servant commanded you. Turn not from it to the right hand or to the left, that you may prosper wherever you go.*
>
> *This Book of the Law shall not depart out of your mouth, but you shall meditate on it day and night, that you may observe and do according to all that is written in it. For then you shall make your way prosperous, and then you shall deal wisely and have good success.*

 What were the Lord's instructions to Joshua in these verses?

 Why was it important for Joshua to follow the instruction of the law (the Word of God), and what did God say the outcome would be if Joshua followed His instructions?

Not long after my powerful encounter with the love of God, God taught me about the importance of meditating on His Word. The lesson came through the sprinkler system that my husband and I had installed in our lawn. One day while looking out the window, I noticed an extraordinary difference in the front lawn and the back lawn. We had installed the system in the front and side lawns only, not the back. I took the responsibility of watering the back lawn.

When I looked out the front window, I noticed that the front lawn looked beautiful and green. When I looked out the back window, I noticed that there were a number of yellow patches, and the back lawn did not look very healthy. I realized that I was falling down on my job of keeping the back lawn watered. The front lawn was being watered regularly, but the back lawn was only being watered sporadically.

While looking at the yellow spots in the back lawn, I heard the Lord say, "If you will diligently and regularly water your life with My Word, your life (like your front lawn) will become green and healthy." It is so valuable for us to spend regular time in the Word of God. Committed, regular time spent meditating in the Word will cause us to prosper. Meditating on God's Word brings refreshing spiritual water to our thirsty souls.

A.W. Tozer tells us in his book *The Pursuit of God*:

> The Spirit-filled walk demands that we live in the Word of God as a fish lives in the sea. By this I do not mean that we study the Bible merely, nor that we take a "course" in Bible doctrine. I mean that we should "meditate day and night" in the sacred Word, that we should love it and feast upon it every hour of the day and night.[1]

The Hebrew word translated meditate in Joshua, chapter 1 is *hagah*, and it means "to murmur...to ponder;—imagine, meditate...mutter, roar...speak, study, talk, utter."[2] The Greek word translated meditate is *meletao*. Vine's Complete Expository

Dictionary of Old and New Testament Words says that *meletao* means primarily *"to care for, ...to attend to, practice, ...be diligent in, ...to ponder, imagine."*³

It is interesting to note how many times that the Hebrew word for meditate refers to talking and speaking. We need to remember the importance of speaking the Word aloud to ourselves as well as studying the Word. As we speak the Word, we plant it in our spirits, and the Word grows and causes us to grow and prosper.

Through Scriptural meditation, our minds are renewed. As we meditate on the Word, our brains are rewired to God's Truths. Scriptural meditation imparts knowledge and wisdom to us. It enables us to see clearly and respond correctly to the situations of life.

We want to make sure that we are caring for and being diligent in the Word. We need to commit time every day to pondering and practicing what the Word says. As we are diligent in studying the Word, and as we practice what we read and study, we are going to see outstanding results.

## 4. Do Not Follow Worldly Counsel—Delight in God's Counsel.

We are given wonderful instructions in Psalm 1:1-3 regarding the value of being diligent to steer clear of worldly influence. At the same time, we are given instructions on the outstanding value of meditating on the Word of God and delighting in its counsel. The psalmist tells us:

> *Blessed (Happy, fortunate, prosperous, and enviable) is the man who walks and lives not in the counsel of the ungodly [following their advice, their plans and purposes], nor stands [submissive and inactive] in the path where sinners walk, or sits down [to relax and rest] where the scornful [and the mockers] gather.*

*But his delight and desire are in the law of the Lord, and on His law (the precepts, the instructions, the teachings of God) he habitually meditates (ponders and studies) by day and by night.*

*And he shall be like a tree firmly planted [and tended] by the streams of water, ready to bring forth its fruit in its season; its leaf also shall not fade or wither; and everything he does shall prosper [and come to maturity].*

**Question:** According to Psalm 1:1, how do we guard our hearts?

**Question:** According to Psalm 1:2, how do we strengthen our hearts?

**Question:** What are we told in verse 3 will happen if we follow the instructions from verses 1-2?

 How have you been blessed as you have spent time meditating on the Word of God?

If we want to truly prosper in life, we need to spend concentrated time meditating on the Word. As we remain dedicated to God's Word, we will learn what to do and how to respond in every situation.

## 5. Guard Your Heart with All Vigilance.

The Word is a powerful source of protection for our lives. We are given important instructions in the following verses regarding the value of guarding out hearts:

> *Keep and guard your heart with all vigilance and above all that you guard, for out of it flow the springs of life (Proverbs 4:23).*
>
> *...For out of the fullness (the overflow, the superabundance) of the heart the mouth speaks. The good man from his inner good treasure flings forth good things, and the evil man out of his inner evil storehouse flings forth evil things (Matthew 12:34-35).*

 According to Proverbs 4:23, why is it important for us to be vigilant in guarding our hearts?

**Question:** What does Jesus tell us about the importance of storing good things in our hearts in Matthew 12:34-35?

**Question:** From the following verses, what are some things we can do to strengthen and fortify our hearts, so that we can store good treasure in our inner storehouse?

- Psalm 13:5-6—

- Psalm 16:7-8—

- Psalm 37:3-6—

- Psalm 52:8-9—

- Psalm 55:22—

- Psalm 91:1-2—

During the period of time that I was diligently spending time in the Word for healing of my emotions, I was very careful about the things that I let into my life. The majority of my time was spent reading and meditating on the Scriptures.

It is always important for us to guard our hearts, but there are times that we need to be extra vigilant. There are things that people say, news broadcasts, and life circumstances that will bring fear and discouragement to us. When discouraging words or life circumstances try to steal our joy and peace, it is very important for us to spend extra time in the Word and presence of God.

It should be our heart's cry to know our Savior intimately. His Word is His invitation to know Him. Through His Word we gain understanding of His nature and His character. As we yield to the Holy Spirit, the rich treasures that are hidden in the Word are uncovered and revealed to us. It is God's sincere desire for each of us to find the deep and profound treasures of Truth in His Word. As we keep our heart pure and open before Him, these truths will be revealed.

If someone speaks negative words to you, simply do not receive them. It is not necessary to say anything, but in your heart do not receive the negative words. When you are alone, rebuke those words in the name of Jesus Christ, and begin to confess that you are resting and trusting in God's love and faithfulness. While we are guarding our hearts from negative words or discouraging circumstances, it is also very important to guard what we say. The words that we speak have the power of life and death (Proverb 18:21). Positive words provide protection for our hearts. Negative words leave our hearts vulnerable.

We need to bring our words into agreement with God's Word. When we speak His Word, strength is imparted to us. In His Word we find life, health, power, hope, peace, joy, comfort, etc. God's Word is the seed of Heavenly life!

**Lesson Application:** Ask the Spirit of the Lord to direct you to passages of Scripture to meditate on this week. Ask the Lord to help you recognize the difference between the wisdom of the world and the wisdom of His Word. Make a commitment to give God's Word priority in your life. Ask the Lord to help you diligently guard your heart. Spend time in the secret place with Him, seeking counsel and direction. Yield yourself completely to the leadership of the Holy Spirit.

*Also he has informed us of your love in the [Holy] Spirit. For this reason we also, from the day we heard of it, have not ceased to pray and make [special] request for you, [asking] that you may be filled with the full (deep and clear) knowledge of His will in all spiritual wisdom [in comprehensive insight into the ways and purposes of God] and in understanding and discernment of spiritual things—*

*That you may walk (live and conduct yourselves) in a manner worthy of the Lord, fully pleasing to Him and desiring to please Him in all things, bearing fruit in every good work and steadily growing and increasing in and by the knowledge of God [with fuller, deeper, and clearer insight, acquaintance, and recognition].*

*[We pray] that you may be invigorated and strengthened with all power according to the might of His glory, [to exercise] every kind of endurance and patience (perseverance and forbearance) with joy." Colossians 1: 8-11*

*Dear Lord,*

*Thank You for helping me to meditate in Your powerful Word day and night. I want to learn how to feast upon Your Word. I want Your Word to saturate my mind, my heart, and my emotions. By the power of your Spirit, give me new revelation and insight each time I read and study the amazing truths recorded in Scripture. Plant Your Word deep in my heart. Help me to diligently guard my heart. Help me to be invigorated and strengthened with Your power, might, and glory. Enable me to prosper in every area of my life.*

*In Jesus' precious name,*

## Notes

*Lesson Three*

# THE POWER OF LOVE

*"Love never fails [never fades out or becomes obsolete or comes to an end]..."*
*1 Corinthians 13:8*

*Lesson Focus:* We will walk in genuine victory as we abide and walk in the love of God.

*Introduction:* We can completely trust in the all-embracing love of God. There is nothing that compares to God's love. His love is so amazing that it holds the universe together. God's love extends beyond human comprehension. It is powerful beyond words. If we want to walk in genuine victory, it is essential to plug into this magnificent source of power. God's love powers the universe, and it is the power source for our very lives. Nothing can stop us when we walk in the love of God.

Our Heavenly Father loves us so much that He sent Jesus to die on the cross for us. Our Savior's love is so amazing that He was willing to suffer and die in our place. The Holy Spirit lovingly guides and helps us in everything we do. God's love is the catalyst to understanding the depths of who He is and all that He has provided for us. There is nothing more powerful than the love of God, and we have the wonderful privilege of abiding and walking in His love moment-by-moment.

The more we comprehend the awesomeness of God's love, the more we will walk in the fullness of all that He desires for us. Paul tells us in 1 Corinthians 13 that love never fails. Therefore, we move out of failure and into victory through abiding in God's love. True success comes through dwelling in the love of God. God's love will enable us to soar to new heights and new levels of revelation in all the magnificent aspects of His nature and character.

**TRUE SUCCESS COMES THROUGH DWELLING IN THE LOVE OF GOD.**

God longs for us to enter into new realms of understanding His will and His ways. Love is an awesome key that gives us access into the wonders of the kingdom of God. When we truly understand the tremendous scope of God's love for us, we will be unstoppable!

Keep in mind that the Word of God is His love letter to us. It is in the Word that we find all the instructions and counsel we need to live successful lives. Through God's Word and His Spirit, He draws us and woos us into sweet communion and fellowship. The more we yield to the Holy Spirit, and the more we abide in the Word, the more we will grasp the fullness of God's marvelous love.

Take some time right now to ask Jesus to immerse you in His love. Ask your Heavenly Father to allow you to experience the richness of His love for you. Ask the Holy Spirit to open the eyes of your heart to all the wonders of God's love. Through the revelation of God's amazing love, you will walk in the splendor and the majesty of all that He desires for you.

# FIVE POWERFUL REASONS TO ABIDE IN THE LOVE OF GOD

## 1. Your Joy and Gladness Will be Full and Complete.

In John 15:9-11, Jesus tells us that we will experience joy and gladness in full measure through faithfulness to His commandments and abiding in His love. In these verses He says:

> *I have loved you, [just] as the Father has loved Me; abide in my love [continue in His love with Me].*
>
> *If you keep My commandments [if you continue to obey My instruction], you will abide in My love and live on in it, just as I have obeyed My Father's commandments and live on in His love.*
>
> *I have told you these things, that My Joy and delight may be in you, and that your joy and gladness may be of full measure and complete and overflowing.*

 According to these verses, how does Jesus love us, and why is it important for us to abide in His love?

 As you consider Jesus' instructions in this passage, why is obedience to God's Word so valuable?

Jesus genuinely wants us to live and dwell in His presence. He wants our whole heart. He wants us to obey Him out of a heart of love. The Greek word translated abide in John 15 is *meno*, and it means "*to stay (in a given place...)...continue, dwell, endure, be present, remain, stand.*"[1]

No matter how difficult it is for us to obey, it is absolutely essential that we continue in the instructions given to us in the Word. It is important for us to listen daily to the counsel of the Holy Spirit. If we want to live victorious lives we must remain faithful to the precepts of God's Word, and we must learn to abide in His love.

We often want to run when things become difficult, but God tells us to endure, to remain, and to stand. There are times when we want to hold on to bitterness and resentment, but God tells us to let go and forgive. He will give us the help we need to obey His counsel and instructions. We are not required to accomplish anything in our own strength. We have a wonderful friend and helper in the Holy Spirit.

God longs to help us step into the fullness of His love. He is always waiting and longing for us to ask for His help and assistance. During the time of emotional struggle that I shared in lesson one, I knew I was not in the will of God. I wanted to obey, but I was struggling to let go and trust God completely. The cry of my heart at that time was, "God, please don't let go of me!"

God waited patiently for me, and He arranged circumstances in my life that led me to pray, "Lord, please make me willing to be willing to do Your will." That was the prayer that God was waiting to hear. When I finally asked for help, God gave me the wisdom and help I needed. It took time, but as I continued to pursue God through His Word and His Spirit, true freedom came, and I entered into new levels of understanding the love of God.

Through our obedience, we will abide in God's love, and our joy and delight will be full and overflowing. The joy of the Lord is our strength (Nehemiah 8:10). When we walk in love and obedience, strength and power are released. We become more than conquerors through the love of God (Romans 8:31-39).

## 2. You Will be Filled With the Fullness of God.

Paul prays a prayer in Ephesians 3:16-19 that gives us valuable understanding of the importance of dwelling in God's love. In these verses Paul prays:

> *May He grant you out of the rich treasury of His glory to be strengthened and reinforced with mighty power in the inner man by the [Holy] Spirit [Himself indwelling your innermost being and personality].*
>
> *May Christ through your faith [actually] dwell (settle down, abide, make His permanent home) in your hearts! May you be rooted deep in love and founded securely on love,*
>
> *That you may have the power and be strong to apprehend and grasp with all the saints [God's devoted people, the experience of that love] what is the breadth and length and height and depth [of it];*
>
> *[That you may really come] to know [practically, through experience for yourselves] the love of Christ, which far surpasses mere knowledge [without experience]; that you may be filled [through all your being] unto all the fullness of God [may have the richest measure of the divine Presence, and become a body wholly filled and flooded with God Himself]!*

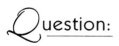 According to Ephesians 3:16-19, how are we strengthened with the power and presence of God?

**Question:** How does Christ make His permanent home in our hearts?

**Question:** According to these verses, why is it important to be rooted deep in the love of God?

From the beginning of time, God has wanted us to live and dwell in His love and the sweetness of His presence. He created us to have sweet fellowship and intimate communion with Him. It is so important for us to receive the words of Paul's prayer in Ephesians 3. We need to pray it over and over until we experience the love of God that surpasses knowledge. We need to daily ask God to enable us to walk in the fullness of His love.

There is nothing more exciting than to be filled to the measure with the fullness of God. It may seem impossible, but Paul tells us in verses 20-21 of Ephesians 3 that it is possible:

> *Now to Him Who, by (inconsequence of) the [action of His] power that is at work within us, is able to [carry out His purpose and] do superabundantly, far over and above all that we [dare] ask or think [infinitely beyond our highest prayers, desires, thoughts, hopes, or dreams]—To Him be glory in the church and in Christ Jesus throughout all generations forever and ever. Amen (so be it).*

## 3. You Will Find Life, Prosperity, and Honor.

It is so important for us to pursue the love of God, along with His righteousness, because there are wonderful benefits that come from this pursuit. We read in Proverbs 21:21:

*He who pursues righteousness and love finds life, prosperity and honor (NIV).*

 According to this verse, how important is walking in righteousness and love?

 How have you experienced the wonderful benefits revealed in this verse as you have pursued God's righteousness and love?

I have never experienced a time when pursuing righteousness and love did not ultimately bring life, prosperity and honor. God always honors and blesses us when we follow His counsel.

There was a time when someone close to me made a decision that I felt could have a very negative outcome for my family. There were individuals involved who I believed were taking unfair advantage in the circumstances surrounding this decision. As I diligently sought the Lord in prayer, He instructed me to walk in love.

The Lord counseled me to honor the decision. He told me that He would bless me as I walked in love. I knew in my heart that

> **WE OPEN A DOOR FOR GOD'S BLESSINGS WHEN WE CHOOSE LOVE.**

I could trust in His faithfulness, and He would bring blessings regardless of the circumstances. My family has been blessed beyond measure since that time. There is never a time when God will not bless us when we yield to His counsel and we walk in His love. We open a door for God's blessings when we choose love.

## 4. You Will Dwell in His Presence, Experiencing His Freedom and Glory.

As we dwell in God's love, we dwell in His presence, and as we dwell in His presence, we continue in His love. We read in 1 John 4:16:

> *And we know (understand, recognize, are conscious of, by observation and by experience) and believe (adhere to and put faith in and rely on) the love God cherishes for us. God is love, and he who dwells and continues in love dwells and continues in God, and God dwells and continues in him.*

Where God's presence dwells there is freedom. Freedom is also found through God's Word (Psalm 119:45). We cannot separate God from His Word, and we cannot separate God from His love. As we dwell in God's Word and we dwell in His love, we dwell in freedom and we reflect His glory. We read in 2 Corinthians 3:17-18:

> *Now the Lord is the Spirit, and where the Spirit of the Lord is, there is liberty (emancipation from bondage, freedom).*
>
> *And all of us, as with unveiled face, [because we] continued to behold [in the Word of God] as in a mirror the glory of the Lord, are constantly being*

*transfigured into His very own image in ever increasing splendor and from one degree of glory to another; [for this comes] from the Lord [Who is] the Spirit.*

**Question:** According to 1 John 4:16, how does God's love dwell in us?

**Question:** According to 2 Corinthians 3:17, what happens when we are filled with God's presence?

**Question:** What happens when we abide in God's presence through His Word and His Spirit (2 Corinthians 3:18)?

Through God's presence in our lives, we are changed into His likeness. As we abide in God's love and in His Word, we experience ever-increasing measures of His glory. God's love, His Word, and His glory are all linked together. The more we dwell in His love and His Word, the more we reflect His glory.

God has chosen to release His glory to the world through those who receive His powerful love by faith. When we walk by faith, trusting in God's promises and the power of His love, we become shining lights in this world. Through faith, we become vessels of God's glory, and we are empowered to share His Word and His love to a world in desperate need of His loving touch. The more we dwell in God's presence, abiding in His love and His Word, the more His light will shine through us.

## 5. Fear Will be Expelled From Your Life.

It is through the Holy Spirit's presence in our lives that we are released from bondage. The anointing of God brings freedom to those who are bound and oppressed (Luke 4:18). The goal of our enemy is to keep us bound in every way possible, and fear is his main weapon. His desire is to keep us so bound by fear that we will be ineffective in our walk of faith. God, however, has a weapon that never fails, and that weapon is His love. John tells us in 1 John 4:18:

> ***There is no fear in love [dread does not exist], but full-grown (complete, perfect) love turns fear out of doors** and **expels every trace of terror! For fear brings with it the thought of punishment, and [so] he who is afraid has not reached the full maturity of love [is not yet grown into love's complete perfection].***

uestion: What does John tell us about God's love in 1 John 4:18?

**uestion:** What attributes of God's love do we find in 1 Corinthians 13:4-8?

**uestion:** How do these attributes of His love enable us to walk free from fear?

Words are inadequate to describe God's patience and loving-kindness. The blood of Jesus wipes away all our sins and record of wrongs. God's love sees our potential, not our failure. He is so understanding and patient with us. One morning, when I was in the midst of my intense emotional battle, the Lord spoke to me out of Isaiah 40:28 saying: *"Do you not know? Have you not heard? The Lord is the everlasting God, the Creator of the ends of the earth. He will not grow tired or weary and his understanding no one can fathom"* (NIV).

I knew that God was telling me that He understood my struggle. Through His loving-kindness, He was graciously making a way for me to walk back into His will. Scripture tells us that the goodness of God leads us to repentance (Romans 2:4). God will always lead us in kindness, mercy and love. No matter what struggle we are in, He is waiting with open arms to help us and receive us into His love.

As God brought healing to my life through His Word and His awesome love, something remarkable happened. I discovered a newfound confidence in everything that I did. I was more confident interacting in difficult situations and with people in general. I was more confident in prayer, and I was more confident to step out in the things that God had gifted me to do.

Charles Spurgeon tells us in his book, *Joy In Christ's Presence*:

> How often have my eyes been full of tears when I have realized the thought that Jesus loves me! How my spirit has been melted within me at the assurance that He thinks of me and carries me in His heart! ... Can you say of yourself, 'He loved me'? (See Galatians 2:20.) Then look down into this sea of love, and try to guess its depth. Does it not stagger your faith that He loves you so? ... Even the angels have never known such love as this! Jesus does not engrave their names upon His hands or call them His bride. No, this highest fellowship he reserves for worms such as ourselves, whose only response is tearful, hearty thanksgiving and love.[2]

When we are able to truly look into the depths of the sea of God's love, nothing will be impossible for us. Through His love, we will fulfill the call of God on our lives, and we will spread His wonderful love everywhere we go.

*Lesson Application:* Ask God to show you any changes that you need to make in your life in order to walk and abide more fully and completely in His love. Begin to cry out to know the breadth and length and height and depth of God's love. Continue seeking and asking until you are filled to the measure with all the fullness of God (Ephesians 3:16-19).

Take time to meditate on the attributes of the Love of God recorded in 1 Corinthians 13:4-8. Meditate on the patience and kindness of the One who does not grow tired or weary. Recognize that He loves and understands you fully and completely, and His love has no boundaries or limits. Understand that the only limits to God's love are the ones we place there.

*"Love endures long and is patient and kind; love never is envious nor boils over with jealousy, is not boastful or vainglorious, does not display itself haughtily. It is not conceited (arrogant and inflated with pride); it is not rude (unmannerly) and does not act unbecomingly. Love (God's love in us) does not insist on its own rights or its own way for it is not self-seeking; it is not touchy or fretful or resentful; it takes no account of the evil done to it [it pays no attention to a suffered wrong]. It does not rejoice at injustice and unrighteousness, but rejoices when right and truth prevail. Love bears up under anything and everything that comes, is ever ready to believe the best of every person, its hopes are fadeless under all circumstances, and it endures everything [without weakening]. Love never fails [never fades out or becomes obsolete or comes to an end]..."*
*1 Corinthians 13:4-8*

*Dear Lord,*

*Help me to know and understand the depths of Your love for me, and help me to walk in the fullness of Your love toward everyone I meet. It is my sincere desire to comprehend the fullness of all the wonderful aspects of Your love—its patience and kindness, its grace and courtesy, its willingness to yield to others, and its willingness to forgive completely. I want to walk in Your love that bears up under anything and everything that comes—love that believes the best of everyone and always hopes and endures everything without weakening. Thank You that Your love never fails!*

*In Jesus' precious name,*

*Amen*

*Lesson Four*

# THE POWER OF OBEDIENCE

*"... As the Scripture says, What eye has not seen and ear has not heard and has not entered into the heart of man, [all that] God has prepared (made and keeps ready) for those who love Him [who hold Him in affectionate reverence, promptly obeying Him and gratefully recognizing the benefits He has bestowed]."*
*1 Corinthians 2:9*

**Lesson Focus:** As we walk in obedience to God's Word and Spirit, we will walk in the wonders and blessings of the kingdom of God.

**Introduction:** When we come to fully understand the wonderful blessings that are released in our lives through walking in obedience, we will cry out for God's help to walk in obedience moment-by-moment, every day of our lives. God does not ask us to obey because He is a hard taskmaster. He asks us to obey because He loves us and longs to bless us. It is His sincere desire to see us walking in the fullness of all that He has provided for us.

As we walk in obedience to God's Word and His Spirit, we have the awesome privilege of moving into realms of His kingdom that can only be accessed through spiritual revelation. Obedience is another powerful key that unlocks the door to the marvelous realm of the Spirit.

> **OBEDIENCE IS ANOTHER POWERFUL KEY THAT UNLOCKS THE DOOR TO THE MARVELOUS REALM OF THE SPIRIT.**

God longs to open our eyes to the marvels of His kingdom, but it is important for us to line our hearts up with His. Just as loving parents withhold blessings and privileges from children because of disobedience, it is the same with God. The sooner the child obeys, the sooner blessings and privileges can be released. The more we walk in God's will, the more the wonders and marvels of His kingdom can be revealed to us.

As we walk in obedience, we will advance to new levels and new realms of walking in the Spirit. Whole new worlds of understanding and revelation will open up to us as we walk in sincere obedience.

God is so rich in mercy and loving kindness that even when we do not obey, He extends His love and kindness to us. It is the kindness of God that leads us to repentance (Romans 2:4). It is important, however, to remember that the fullness of the blessings of God can only be released through our obedience.

God always gives us the ability to obey. He never asks us to do something without giving us the ability to do what He asks of us. Our Father is completely loving and trustworthy. Our wonderful Savior made total provision for us at the cross. The Holy Spirit is our faithful helper and friend. This dynamic trio will empower and equip us with everything we need to walk in obedience, and they will do it with great kindness and love.

In this lesson we are going to look at some valuable keys to walking in obedience. As we earnestly seek God, He will help us move into the realm of His Spirit where obedience is second nature to us. As we continually yield to Him, with humble and submitted hearts, obedience will be our natural response. There will always be times when it is more difficult to obey than others, but there will never be a time when God will not empower and help us walk in complete submission to His will and plan for our lives.

# SIX VALUABLE KEYS TO WALKING IN OBEDIENCE

## 1. Diligently Follow God's Word.

Moses told the Israelites in Deuteronomy 5:32-33:

> *Therefore you shall be careful to do as the Lord your God has commanded you; you shall not turn aside to the right hand or to the left.*
>
> *You shall walk in all the ways which the Lord your God has commanded you, that you may live and that it may be well with you, and that you may prolong your days in the land which you shall possess* (NKJV).

 According to this passage, what is the result of obedience to the Word of God?

The Lord tells us in Proverbs 1:33:

> *But whoso hearkens to me [Wisdom] shall dwell securely and in confident trust and shall be quiet, without fear or dread of evil.*

**Question:** According to Proverbs 1:33, what is the result of listening to the voice of the Lord?

**Question:** What are the results of following the voice and counsel of God in the following verses?

- Psalm 92:12-15—

- Psalm 112:1-6—

- Psalm 128:1-4—

The voice of Wisdom in Scripture is the voice of Jesus. Jesus is the fulfillment of the Scriptures (Matt. 5:17). He is the living Word of God (John 1:1; 1:14), and He gives us all the ability and strength we need to follow His Word, both Old and New Testament. As we diligently listen and obey, we can completely trust in His faithfulness.

Jesus won the victory over sin and death (1 Cor. 15:57), and He sent the Holy Spirit to empower us to walk in the victory that He purchased for us (John 14:16-17). He has given us everything we need for life and godliness (2 Peter 1:3). As we meditate on His precepts and promises, obeying His counsel, we will walk in the fullness of all that He desires for us.

Jesus makes an awesome promise in John 15:7, when He tells us, *"If you remain in me and my words remain in you, ask whatever you wish, and it will be given you."* This is outstanding! When we obey Jesus' words, we will see our heart's desires fulfilled.

## 2. Recognize the Importance of the Holy Spirit.

The Holy Spirit gives life to the Word of God, and He enables us to walk in its truths. One of His names is the Spirit of Truth. Jesus gives us valuable insight regarding the importance of the Holy Spirit in helping us understand God's truths in the following verses:

> *But when He, the Spirit of Truth (the Truth-giving Spirit) comes, He will guide you into all the Truth (the whole, full Truth)...(John 16:13).*
>
> *Sanctify them [purify, consecrate, separate them for Yourself, make them holy] by Truth; Your Word is Truth (John 17:17).*
>
> *He has made us competent as ministers of a new covenant—not of the letter but of the Spirit; for the letter kills, but the Spirit gives life (2 Cor. 3:6 NIV).*

**Question:** According to John 16:13, how does the Holy Spirit guide us?



**Question:** According to John 17:17, where do we find Truth?

uestion: What do we find in 2 Corinthians 3:6, regarding the importance of the Holy Spirit in our understanding Truth and following it?

The Holy Spirit is Truth. He authored the Word, and as we yield to Him, He will give us revelation into its marvelous truths. We read in Hebrews 4:12 that the Word of God is living and active. Through the Word of God and the Spirit of God, we are privileged to experience a continual flow of the life of God. Abiding in the Word of God and yielding to the Spirit of God will enable us to walk in obedient trust and faith in God.

As we faithfully walk in the truths and precepts of God's Word, we will know the will of God. Therefore, we will know the right response in every situation. Depression and discouragement cannot abide in us when we walk in Truth because God's Truth sets us free (John 8:31-32). The more we understand the freedom that comes to us through obedience to the Word, the more we will desire to genuinely surrender to God's will in every situation of our lives.

## 3. Turn to the Lord with All Your Heart.

Moses told the Israelites in Deuteronomy 30:8-10:

> *And you shall return and obey the voice of the Lord and do all His commandments which I command you today.*
>
> *And the Lord your God will make you abundantly prosperous in every work of your hand, in the fruit of your body, of your cattle, of your land, for good; for the Lord will again delight in prospering you, as He took delight in your fathers.*

***If you obey the voice of the Lord your God, to keep His commandments and His statutes which are written in this Book of the Law, and if you turn to the Lord your God with all your [mind and] heart and with all your being.***

 According to Deuteronomy 30:8-10, what happens when we obey the voice of the Lord, and we turn to Him with all of our heart and with all our being?

 What has God done for you as you have turned to Him with all your heart and with all your being?

God delights in prospering us in every area of our lives. He will prosper us in our jobs, in our families, in finances, in properties, and everything that concerns us as we turn to Him with all our heart and soul. This is not at all difficult for God. He holds the world in His hands (1 Cor. 10:26).

Jesus came to free us from bondage. He came to free us from everything that would hinder us from fully following God's perfect will for our lives. He sent the Holy Spirit to strengthen and empower us to yield to Him with our whole heart. We have been given all the help we need to walk in complete obedience. Our part is to listen, yield, and obey.

As we focus our attention on the Word of God, and we yield to the Holy Spirit, we will find all the wisdom, counsel, and instruction we need. He is waiting with open arms to embrace us. He longs to give us the help and support we need.

## 4. Make a Quality Decision to Obey.

God told the Israelites that it was their choice to walk in His blessings through obedience. God longed to bless them, but the decision was theirs. We read in Deut. 30:19-20:

> *I call heaven and earth to witness this day against you, that I have set before you life and death, the blessing and the curse; therefore choose life, that you and your descendants may live*
>
> *And may love the Lord your God, obey His voice, and cling to Him. For He is your life and the length of your days, that you may dwell in the land which the Lord swore to give to your fathers, to Abraham, Isaac, and Jacob.*

 What instructions did Moses give the children of Israel in this passage?

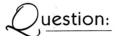 According to this passage, how important are the choices we make?

In Deuteronomy 28, we find the blessings for obedience that God promised to the children of Israel if they would be faithful to His commandments. We also find the curses they would encounter if they walked in disobedience to His Word. We are very blessed as new covenant believers because Jesus redeemed us from the curse of the Law (Galatians 3:13). He redeemed us to walk in the blessings of God.

> **AS WE FOLLOW GOD'S VOICE, WE CAN WALK IN THE FULLNESS OF HIS BLESSINGS.**

As we follow God's voice, we can walk in the fullness of His blessings.

It is important for us to remember that the choice to follow the Holy Spirit's leadership is ours. When we trust and rest in Him, we will be blessed. When we choose to make the Most High our refuge, we will know His faithfulness. As we call upon Him, He will be with us in times of trouble, and He will deliver and honor us (Psalm 91).

There will always be times of testing where the enemy attempts to destroy our faith. Tests and trials do not mean that we have stepped out of God's will. Even when we are seeking to walk in complete submission to God, we will still face tests and trials. At those times, it is important to remember that God *"holds victory in store for the upright"* (Proverbs 2:7 NIV).

God brings maturity to our lives through tests and trials (James 1:2-4). When we are yielded to God, He will enable us to come through victoriously. It may not look like victory during the trial, but ultimately, we will see the good that God brings to us as we stand in faith through the tests and trials. When we make a quality decision to obey, no matter how difficult the circumstance, we will be blessed.

## 5. Live a Yielded Life of Faith and Trust.

Paul tells us in Galatians 2:20:

*I have been crucified with Christ [in Him I have shared His crucifixion]; it is no longer I who live, but Christ (the Messiah) lives in me; and the life I now live in the body I live by faith in (by adherence to and reliance on and complete trust in) the Son of God, Who loved me and gave Himself up for me.*

**Question:** According to Galatians 2:20, how are we to live?

**Question:** According to the following verses, what are some ways for us to live yielded lives of faith and trust?

- Acts 4:31—

- Ephesians 4:2-3—

- 2 Peter 1:5-7—

- 1 John 1:9—

- 1 John 2:27—

When we have been crucified with Christ, we are no longer in charge of our lives. He is in charge. Therefore, it is important for us to yield ourselves completely to Him. As we pray, God will be faithful to hear and answer us. As we humble ourselves before Him, He will support and strengthen us.

I often pray, "Lord, I yield myself to You. I yield my mind, my will, and my emotions to You. I choose to walk by faith. I am resting and trusting in You." Sometimes I simply say over and over in my mind, "I yield to You Lord. I yield to You." Praying in this way enables me to refocus my thoughts. It allows the Holy Spirit to take charge of my emotions.

> WHEN WE LIVE A CRUCIFIED LIFE, WE WILL BE VICTORIOUS.

When we live a crucified life, we will be victorious. As we daily yield to God's will, He will enable us to do what is right. When we reach the Galatians 2:20 level of faith, the fiery darts our enemies send our way will be ineffective.

## 6. Make Sure that Your Heart Remains Soft and Trusting.

We are told in Hebrews 3:15, 19:

> *Then while it is [still] called Today, if you would hear His voice* and *when you hear it, do not harden your hearts as in the rebellion [in the desert, when the people provoked and irritated and embittered God against them]….*
> *So we see that they were not able to enter [into His rest], because of their unwillingness to adhere to* and *trust in* and *rely on God [unbelief had shut them out].*

**Question:** According to these verses, how important is it for us to keep our hearts soft and responsive to the Word and counsel of God?

**Question:** How has hearing, trusting, and believing in God's Word enabled you to enter into His rest?

When I became aware of the power of God's Word to bring victory and freedom to my life, I started underlining Scripture promises and verses that were meaningful and encouraging to me. Through these verses, God has enabled me to keep my heart soft and trusting. When a difficultly arises in my life, I open my Bible and begin to read underlined verses. I often go to the Psalms, and I stay there until I find myself in the verses I am reading. It is not hard because the writers of the Psalms experienced many difficulties.

God began to impress upon my heart the importance of trusting in His Word, over the circumstances of life, many years ago. Paul tells us in 1 Corinthians 5:7, *"We live by faith, not by sight"* (NIV). We cannot build our faith on what we see in the natural realm. We must trust in the Word of God. We read in Romans 10:17, *"So then faith comes by hearing and hearing by the word of God"* (NKJV).

During times of trial, it is important that we do not let difficult circumstances move us into fear, resentment, unbelief, etc. These are the opposite of faith. When we are fearful or resentful, we are not trusting in God's faithfulness. When we are not resting and trusting, we are in disobedience to God's Word that continually instructs us to rest and trust and walk in faith.

We obey God through resting and trusting in His Word. When difficult circumstances bring fear and discouragement, it is so important to seek understanding from God. We do not want to respond in fear, doubt, or unbelief. We want to obey God's commands not to fear or become anxious.

A friend called me one afternoon, and she shared that a tragic accident had happened to someone I knew. At that time, I was new in my faith walk. I wasn't a new Christian, but I was new in learning to truly trust God with every detail of my life. The call brought a lot of fear to me.

Before I went to sleep that night, I asked God to help me let go of the fear that had come to me through hearing about the accident. When I woke up the next morning, the Spirit of the Lord led me to open my Bible to the book of Proverbs. He then led me to verses that I had underlined. Through these verses the fear lifted. That morning, I read the following verses from the NIV Bible:

> Proverbs 1:33: *"But whoever listens to me will live in safety and be at ease, without fear of harm."*
>
> Proverbs 2:7-8: *"He holds victory in store for the upright... and protects the way of His faithful ones."*
>
> Proverbs 3:25-26: *"Have no fear of sudden disaster...for the Lord will be your confidence and will keep your foot from being snared."*
>
> Proverbs 14:26: *"He who fears the Lord has a secure fortress, and for his children it will be a refuge."*

After reading these verses, the fear and discouragement completely lifted. When we hear bad or discouraging news, it is so important that we go to the Lord for encouragement. No matter how difficult a situation, God will make a way for us. He will comfort us as well as those who are in need of His comfort. He will be our strong tower in every situation. As we hear, listen, and obey the truths of Scripture, we will have perfect peace.

I am not saying that there will not be periods of grief. But I am saying that we can always trust in God's faithfulness. We can receive His words of comfort. We can trust in the knowledge that He is holding victory in store for us, and He provides protection for us.

We can know with certainty that God is always working for our good (Romans 8:28). He will use every trial and difficulty in our lives to make us a blessing to others. Through trials and difficulties, He works compassion and understanding in us that we are able to offer to others who need comfort and compassion.

It is so important that we trust God, no matter what. He will always give us help and support. When we trust in God, we are walking in obedience to His commands. If we will trust and obey, recognizing that God knows what is best, we will be victorious.

God's precepts and promises will restore peace and joy and hope. The promises and instructions of the Word will bring us freedom, and they will enable our faith to remain stable and fixed. I have seen this happen time and time again. As I have kept my heart focused on the truths of God's Word, He has kept my heart soft, and He has brought me through to victory every time. When I go my own way, it never works. There may be some temporary fulfillment when I go my own way, but it never lasts. Only God's ways bring lasting fulfillment.

I mentioned in the introduction to this lesson that obedience moves us into deeper realms of the Spirit of God. We do not want to miss anything that God desires for us. If we will obey, we will see the goodness and glory of God. It happened time and time again in the Scriptures, and it will happen in our lives.

*The Power of Obedience*

 Take some time this week to meditate on the blessings of God recorded in Deuteronomy 28:1-14. Thank Him for redeeming you from the curse of the Law that is recorded in the remaining verses of Deuteronomy 28. Make a commitment that you are going to listen to God's voice. Determine that you are going to walk in obedience to His Word and His Will, through the power and help of the Holy Spirit. Resolve in your heart that you are going to trust and obey.

*"If you will listen diligently to the voice of the Lord your God, being watchful to do all His commandments...all these blessings shall come upon you and overtake you... Blessed shall you be in the city and blessed shall you be in the field...The Lord will cause your enemies who rise up against you to be defeated before your face: they will come against you one way and flee before you seven ways...And the Lord shall make you have a surplus of prosperity...The Lord shall make you the head, and not the tail; and you shall be above only, and you shall not be beneath..."*

*Selected verses from Deuteronomy 28:1-13*

*Dear Lord,*

*Thank You for leading me and guiding me in the Truth of Your Word. Thank You for Your powerful presence in my life. Soften my heart daily, and help me to be sensitive to Your voice. I genuinely desire to walk in Your will and Your plans for my life. I am so grateful for the incredible blessings You bring to my life through the wonderful precepts of Your Word. Thank You for helping me to listen, submit, trust and obey!*

*In Jesus' precious name,*

# GOD WILL GIVE YOU STRENGTH AND POWER

*"He gives power to the faint and weary, and to him who has no might He increases strength [causing it to multiply and making it to abound]. Even youths shall faint and be weary, and [selected] young men shall feebly stumble and fall exhausted; But those who wait for the Lord [who expect, look for, and hope in Him] shall change and renew their strength and power; they shall lift their wings and mount up [close to God] as eagles [mount up to the sun]; they shall run and not be weary, they shall walk and not faint or become tired."*
Isaiah 40:29-31

**Lesson Focus:** As we yield to the Spirit of God and the Word of God, He gives us all the strength and power we need to accomplish everything He has called us to accomplish.

**Introduction:** In this lesson we will build on the powerful truths we have discussed in preceding lessons. As we abide in God's Word, and we walk in love and obedience, yielding to the Holy Spirit, we will have all the strength we need to live successful lives. As we wait on the Lord, placing our hope in Him, He renews our strength. He gives us spiritual strength to run and not grow weary. He empowers us to walk in faith so that we do not faint or become tired, no matter how difficult the circumstances of our lives.

In the natural realm we grow weary and we become tired, but there is a place in the spirit realm were we mount up as eagles. When we place our trust in God, He makes a way for us to soar in the Spirit. God gives power to those who have no might. When we wait on Him, He causes our strength to multiply and abound.

> GOD GIVES POWER TO THOSE WHO HAVE NO MIGHT. WHEN WE WAIT ON HIM, HE CAUSES OUR STRENGTH TO MULTIPLY AND ABOUND.

God gives us ability and power to do what He calls us to do. Jesus promised us that he would always be with us. He also promised us that he would send the Spirit of Truth to help us. The Holy Spirit empowered Jesus for ministry, and He will empower and enable us to walk in God's will for our lives. He will give us all the strength we need.

The Holy Spirit gives us revelation regarding the Word of God. He authored the Word, and He gives us understanding of all its powerful precepts and instructions. As we have discussed previously, there is incredible power in the truths we find in God's Word, and there is incredible power available to us through the Holy Spirit. God has given us everything we need to live successful, victorious, amazing lives.

# FOUR VALUABLE KEYS TO WALKING IN STRENGTH AND POWER

## 1. Recognize that God's Word is Alive and Full of Power.

In Hebrews 4:12 we are told about the extraordinary power of God's Word to change our lives. The Scripture tell us:

> *For the Word that God speaks is alive and full of power [making it active, operative, energizing, and effective]; it is sharper than any two-edged sword, penetrating to the dividing line of the breath of life (soul) and [the immortal] spirit, and of joints and marrow [of the deepest parts of our nature], exposing and sifting and analyzing and judging the very thoughts and purposes of the heart.*

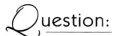 According to Hebrews 4:12, why is God's Word full of power?

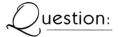 How have you experienced God's Word sifting and analyzing your thoughts?

When I read through the Bible for healing of my emotions, I experienced the power of the Word exposing, sifting, analyzing, and judging the thoughts and purposes of my heart. As I was reading through Scripture, I made decisions that I was going to do what the Word instructed me to do.

As my heart changed, my actions changed. The Word was penetrating the deepest parts of me. It was as if a master surgeon began to cut out the wrong patterns of thinking that had been holding me in bondage. The Word was dividing between my soul (my mind, will, and emotions) and my born-again spirit. The more I filled my life with truths from God's Word, the stronger I became in my spirit. The Truth of God's Word began to win the victory over the wrong thinking in my soul.

## 2. Recognize the Importance of the Holy Spirit.

Before Jesus ascended to heaven, He gave instructions to His disciples to wait for the Holy Spirit to empower them for ministry. Jesus told them in Acts 1:8:

> *But you shall receive power (ability, efficiency, and might) when the Holy Spirit has come upon you, and you shall be My witnesses in Jerusalem and all Judea and Samaria and to the ends (the very bounds) of the earth.*

Lets take a look at the following definitions:

| | |
|---|---|
| POWER | capacity to do something, strength... authority to act...persuasiveness, |
| ABILITY | being able, intelligence or competence, natural gift for something |
| EFFICIENCY | competence, productive use of resources... |
| MIGHT | great power, physical strength[1] |

 As you consider these definitions, what did Jesus promise us in Acts 1:8 regarding the work of the Holy Spirit in our lives?

Jesus promised his followers that He would not leave them helpless. He told them that He would send them the Holy Spirit to strengthen and help them. In John 14:15-18 He tells us:

> *If you [really] love Me, you will keep (obey) My commands.*
>
> *And I will ask the Father, and He will give you another Comforter (Counselor, Helper, Intercessor, Advocate, Strengthener, and Standby), that He may remain with you forever—*
>
> *The Spirit of Truth, Whom the world cannot receive (welcome, take to its heart), because it does not see Him or know and recognize Him. But you know and recognize Him, for He lives with you [constantly] and will be in you.*
>
> *I will not leave you as orphans [comfortless, desolate, bereaved, forlorn, helpless]; I will come [back] to you.*

 According to this passage, how dependable is the Holy Spirit?

uestion: What happened in the following passages of Scripture from the book of Acts regarding the strength and power imparted through the Holy Spirit?

- Acts 4:13—

- Acts 4:29-31—

- Acts 5:14-16—

- Acts 6:8-10—

- Acts 8:6-8—

In the days and weeks following my encounter with the outpouring of God's love, I noticed that I had received a new confidence and boldness. One of the amazing results of my encounter was a greater ease and ability to talk about the things of God.

I also began to see some amazing answers to prayer as I prayed for friends and family. God began to give me understanding and wisdom to give wise counsel that I knew could only have come from Him. I was in awe of the things that God revealed to me.

One day while I was vacuuming, I began to have thoughts about a friend of mine, and God began to give me some clear insight regarding her life. About 10 minutes later, she called on the phone. I had not talked to her in weeks.

When she began to share the struggle that she was experiencing, I knew exactly what to tell her. I told her what had happened while I was vacuuming. She was amazed, and she followed the revelation

I had received from the Lord. She was so blessed that God would speak to someone about her situation that she began attending church again. She had been out of church for a long time, but the experience changed her life in a dramatic way. As she followed the counsel from the Lord, her situation completely changed.

## 3. Understand the Authority and Power that Jesus Gives to Us.

Jesus told his followers in Luke 10:19-20:

> *Behold! I have given you authority and power to trample upon serpents and scorpions, and [physical and mental strength and ability] over all the power that the enemy [possesses]; and nothing shall in any way harm you.*
>
> *Nevertheless, do not rejoice at this, that the spirits are subject to you, but rejoice that your names are enrolled in heaven.*

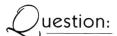 What did Jesus tell us we have the ability to do, and what did He promise us in Luke 10:19?

 What instruction did He give us in verse 20? Why do you think He added this statement?

In John 14:12-14, Jesus gave us power to use His name:

*I assure you, most solemnly I tell you, if anyone steadfastly believes in Me, he will himself be able to do the things that I do; and he will do even greater things than these, because I go to the Father.*

*And I will do [I Myself will grant] whatever you ask in My Name [as presenting all that I AM], so that the Father may be glorified and extolled in (through) the Son.*

*[Yes] I will grant [I Myself will do for you] whatever you shall ask in My Name [as presenting all that I AM] (John 14:12-14).*

**Question:** According to John 14:12-14, how much power do we have in the name of Jesus?

**Question:** Why has Jesus imparted such power to us (v. 13)?

Jesus has authorized and empowered us to use His name. In His name, we represent Him and all that He is. Through steadfast faith and belief in Him, we can do miraculous things. We have the authority and power to trample our enemy. We have physical and mental strength and ability over all the power of the enemy. Therefore, we never need to fear.

Once we make Jesus our Savior and Lord, everywhere we go, we walk in His authority. The more we understand this awesome authority, the more we will see these promises fulfilled. As we exercise our faith, we will see remarkable things. We represent the King of Kings and the Lord of Lords. This is outstanding. We need to continually remind ourselves that we have been given strength and power in the mighty name of Jesus Christ.

## 4. Understand the Power of Submitting and Resisting.

We are told in James 4:7:

> *Submit yourselves, then, to God. Resist the devil, and he will flee from you (NIV).*

 According to James 4:7, what do we need to do when our enemy comes against us?

 What are some things that you do in order to stay submitted to God?

 Have you resisted the devil in Jesus' name? What was the result?

When our son Michael was 20 years old, he began to struggle with intense anxiety. There were many spiritual weapons that he learned to use to fight these attacks of anxiety. One of the weapons was the instructions from James 4:7.

One night he came under a heavy attack. While I was praying for him, God brought to mind James 4:7. I shared the verse with Michael, and I asked him if his heart was submitted to God. He asked me what he needed to do. I encouraged him to confess any sin that the Holy Spirit brought to mind, and then ask for God's forgiveness.

I also encouraged him to ask the Lord if there was anyone that he needed to forgive. Michael had spent time a number of weeks prior to that night making a list of people he needed to forgive. At that time, he went through his list, and he forgave each one that God revealed to him.

Michael closed his eyes and silently asked the Lord to reveal any area where he needed to let go and submit to God. He opened his eyes a few minutes later, and he told me that his heart was submitted. I did not ask him any questions. I simply encouraged him to begin to resist the devil in the authority of Jesus' name. He did, and the anxiety lifted. A wonderful battle against anxiety was won that night. The attack had been very intense.

The Lord taught Michael many amazing lessons during the time that he battled anxiety. However, no matter what weapon he used, he understood that submission to God was essential in every battle.

When we are battling discouragement or fear or anything else, it is good to say, "Lord, I am resting and trusting in You. I yield to you. Thank you for Your faithfulness." We need to continue submitting to God, and resisting whatever is trying to come against us, until there is peace in our thoughts and peace in our bodies.

I have determined that I am not going to receive the discouragement that the enemy attempts to send my way. Jesus has given every believer power and authority over every assignment of the enemy to bring discouragement or harm. I have seen God's faithfulness time and time again, and I know that He is completely trustworthy in every situation.

There may be times that it looks like the enemy is winning. However, God always has a way of turning the worst situations around for our good and for His glory.

*Lesson Application:* Ask God to help you to walk in greater measures of His power and authority. Ask Him to empower you by His Spirit to accomplish His will for your life. Ask Him if there are any areas of your life where you are not fully submitted to Him. Take some time to submit your life completely to God. Then begin to resist discouragement, fear, anxiety, worry, etc. Simply say, "I refuse to be discouraged, fearful, anxious, etc. in the mighty name of Jesus Christ!" Begin to confess, "I have power, authority, and strength through the power of God's Word, His Name, and His Spirit."

*"I have strength for all things in Christ Who empowers me [I am ready for anything and equal to anything through Him Who infuses inner strength into me; I am self-sufficient in Christ's sufficiency]." Philippians 4:13*

*Dear Lord,*

*Please help me to yield to You every day. I know that it is only through Your strength and power that I am able to walk in Your will and Your way. I want Your Word to be planted deep in my heart—sifting, judging and analyzing the thoughts and motives of my heart. I want Your Spirit to lead me and guide me every step of the way. Empower me with the power of Your Spirit. Fill me with the fullness of Your presence.*

*In Jesus' precious name,*

*Amen*

*Lesson Six*

# EXPERIENCING GOD'S ABUNDANT JOY

*"And the ransomed of the Lord shall return and come to Zion with singing, and everlasting joy shall be upon their heads; they shall obtain joy and gladness, and sorrow and sighing shall flee away."*
*Isaiah 35:10*

**Lesson Focus:** We need to diligently seek the joy of the Lord. It is the distinguishing mark of the victorious Christian life.

**Introduction:** Even during the most difficult times of our lives we can walk in joy because the joy of the Lord does not come from outward circumstances. It comes from within us. It is the fruit of the Spirit of God. Jesus told us if we were thirsty we could come to Him, and as we believed in Him, streams of living water would flow from our innermost being (John 7:37-38). Joy flows naturally from the life-giving spiritual water that Jesus imparts to us.

We are told in Isaiah 35 that the ransomed of the Lord will return with singing, and they will have everlasting joy. This is God's promise to all who believe. We are the ransomed of the Lord. Jesus redeemed us at the cross. When we receive the living water that He gives to us, we obtain joy and gladness. We do not have to live with regret or sorrow. Jesus has borne our griefs and carried our sorrows (Isaiah 53:4). He has opened the door into everlasting joy.

Joy is a powerful spiritual force. It imparts strength to us. We read in Nehemiah 8:10, *"... be not grieved and depressed, for the joy of the Lord is your strength and stronghold."* Joy brings strength to our spirit, our soul, and our body. If we are going to be strong in the Lord, it is absolutely essential that we receive from the life-giving flow of the joy of the Lord.

Joy is an excellent source of healing. We read in Proverbs 17:22, *"A happy heart is good medicine and a cheerful mind works healing."* In this verse we also discover that *"a broken spirit dries up the bones."* It is so important to get in the flow of God's living water that brings joy and refreshing to us spiritually, emotionally, and physically.

Joy enables us to abide in a place of blessing. We are told in Proverbs 15:15, *"He who has a glad heart has a continual feast [regardless of circumstances]."* If we want to enjoy a continual feast, it is important for us to walk in the joy of the Lord.

True joy comes from knowing that we are loved and accepted by God. It comes from knowing our Savior and understanding the complete forgiveness He purchased for us at the cross. It comes from knowing that God is good and kind and completely trustworthy. Our hearts cannot help but overflow with joy when we realize the amazing love that God has for us.

As we have seen in previous lessons, joy is released through abiding in Jesus. As we live in His love and we walk in His instructions, His joy and delight will overflow in our lives. Ask God to help you tap into His amazing joy. It is so important that we tap into the joy that releases God's wonderful life and healing to us. As we walk in joy, the world will see that God is good. Through the joy that flows from our lives, the lives of the people we meet will be refreshed, and God will be glorified.

# SIX VALUABLE KEYS TO WALKING IN JOY

## 1. Joy is Released Through the Anointing of the Holy Spirit.

A wonderful aspect of the anointing of the Spirit of God on a believer's life is joy. In Luke chapter 4, Jesus reads from the scroll of the prophet Isaiah, and He tells the people that He is the fulfillment of the prophecy He just read to them. When we go to the book of Isaiah, we find an expanded version of the prophecy. We read in Isaiah 61:1-3:

> *THE SPIRIT of the Lord God is upon me, because the Lord has anointed and qualified me to preach the Gospel of good tidings to the meek, the poor, and afflicted; He has sent me to bind up and heal the brokenhearted, to proclaim liberty to the [physical and spiritual] captives and the opening of the prison and of the eyes to those who are bound.*
>
> *To proclaim the acceptable year of the Lord [the year of His favor] and the day of vengeance of our God, to comfort all who mourn.*
>
> *To grant [consolation and joy] to those who mourn in Zion—to give them an ornament (a garland or diadem) of beauty instead of ashes, the oil of joy instead of mourning, the garment [expressive] of praise instead of a heavy, burdened, and failing spirit—that they may be called oaks of righteousness [lofty, strong, and magnificent, distinguished for uprightness, justice, and right standing with God], the planting of the Lord, that He may be glorified.*

**Question:** What kind of Gospel was Jesus anointed to preach (v. 1)?

**Question:** Who did Jesus come to comfort (v. 2)?

**Question:** What did Jesus come to impart to us, and what was His purpose in imparting these wonderful blessings (v. 3)?

Jesus came to bless us and make us a blessing. Joyful people are an awesome blessing everywhere they go. I recently re-watched the movie Pollyanna on a classic movie channel. It was one of my childhood favorites. In the movie, an entire town is changed and touched by one little girl who brings the message of love and gladness to a town where it is desperately needed. Our world desperately needs to experience love and joy. These wonderful aspects of the fruit of the Spirit that Pollyanna brings to the town of Harrington are what make the movie so special.

I have known precious people who are like Pollyanna. They spread love and joy everywhere they go. They are true world changers. This amazing ability comes from the Spirit of God. God longs for us to be vessels of His joy and love.

Wouldn't it be wonderful to know that you are a blessing everywhere you go because of the anointing of joy on your life?

Wouldn't it be remarkable to be called an oak of righteousness because you walk in the joy of the Lord? From Isaiah 61, we find that the same anointing which imparts joy also imparts beauty. Have you noticed that there is a beauty that radiates from joyful people? Joy and beauty are amazing benefits of the flow of living water and the anointing that comes from the Spirit of God.

> JOY AND BEAUTY ARE AMAZING BENEFITS OF THE FLOW OF LIVING WATER AND THE ANOINTING THAT COMES FROM THE SPIRIT OF GOD.

## 2. Joy is Imparted Through the Word of God.

We have seen in previous lessons that following the counsel and instruction of the Word enables us to prosper. There is great joy to be received from the precepts and promises of God's Word. David and Jeremiah tell us:

> *The precepts of the Lord are right, rejoicing the heart; the commandment of the Lord is pure and bright, enlightening the eyes (Psalm 19:8).*

> *Your words were found, and I ate them; and Your words were to me a joy and the rejoicing of my heart, for I am called by Your name, O Lord God of hosts (Jeremiah 15:16).*

**Question:** What did David tell us in Psalm 19:8, regarding the precepts of the Lord?

**Question:** What happened when Jeremiah found God's words (Jer. 15:16)?

**Question:** How do the following verses encourage us to receive and maintain joy in our lives?

• Psalm 33:1-4—

• Psalm 40:1-3—

• Psalm 51:10-12—

• Psalm 97:11-12—

When we are discouraged, it is so helpful to meditate on the precepts and promises of God's Word. He has given us counsel and instruction in His Word that will speak to every dilemma and problem we face. It is His will and His plan to heal our broken hearts and release abundant joy in our lives. The truths and promises found in Scripture will put a sparkle in our eyes and joy in our hearts.

## 3. Joy is a Benefit of Walking in Love and Obedience.

As we have seen in previous lessons, joy is a wonderful benefit of walking in love and obedience. It will be good to review Jesus' words from John 15:10-11:

*If you keep My commandment [if you continue to obey My instruction], you will abide in My love and live on in it, just as I have obeyed My Father's commandments and live on in His love.*

*I have told you these things, that My joy and delight may be in you, and that your joy and gladness may be of full measure and complete and overflowing.*

 Why is it important for us to obey Jesus' commandments and live in His love?

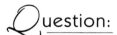 Have you found that obeying Jesus' commandments and living in His love has brought joy and gladness to your life?

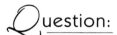 What have you experienced when you step out of obedience?

If we do not walk in obedience, the result will be fear and frustration. These things always rob us of joy. If we refuse to obey in the area of forgiveness, there will be bitterness and resentment. The list goes on and on. True and lasting joy comes through abiding in God's love and walking in obedience to His will and plans for our lives. He is the only one who knows what is best for us. We find true joy and contentment as we surrender to God's will.

I shared in lesson two of this study the result of my letting go of bitterness and resentment. I knew that it was God's will to forgive. When I made the decision to obey God, I experienced His love in a profound way. At the same time, I also experienced overflowing joy. When I determined that I was going to walk in obedience to God's Word, I was released into new levels of His love and His joy.

To this day, I am continually checking to make sure that I am walking in obedience. It is so important for me to walk in God's love. We want to continually be in a place of giving and receiving God's love. We want to make sure we are in the center of His will. When we walk in love and obedience, Jesus has promised us that His joy will overflow in our lives. He will help us every step of the way.

## 4. In God's Presence is Fullness of Joy.

We read in Psalm 16:8-9, 11:

*I have set the Lord continually before me; because he is at my right hand, I shall not be moved.*

*Therefore my heart is glad and my glory [my inner self] rejoices; my body too shall rest and confidently dwell in safety...*

*You will show me the path of life; in Your presence is fullness of joy, at Your right hand there are pleasures forevermore.*

*Question:* What does David tell us about the importance of the presence of the Lord in Psalm 16?

*Experiencing God's Abundant Joy*

**Question:** From the following verses, what are some things that we can do in order to enter into God's presence?

- Psalm 95:1-2—

- Psalm 95:6—

- Psalm 100:1-2—

- Psalm 100:4-5—

- Luke 10:39, 41-42—

There are many exciting ways to enter into God's presence. We enter into His presence through worship, singing, thanksgiving and prayer. We enter into His presence through sitting and listening to His voice as Mary did in Luke 10. Joy is released in our lives through the revelation and understanding we receive while sitting in God's presence.

I have been privileged to experience God's presence through laughter many times. At totally unexpected moments I have laughed and laughed at the simplest things. In those moments, I know that God is releasing His joyful streams of life to me. I have been told when we laugh, endorphins are released in our brains that promote health. They work as natural antidepressants.

God loves to release joy to us in fun-loving ways. Spending time in God's presence brings wonderful satisfaction and joy. God's joyful presence releases amazing healing and strength. In His presence there are *"pleasures forevermore."*

## 5. Be Filled with the Spirit.

Paul instructs us in Ephesians 5:18:

*And do not get drunk with wine, for that is debauchery; but ever be filled and stimulated with the [Holy] Spirit.*

Here we are given the exhortation to always be filled with the Spirit. The Holy Spirit will completely fill and satisfy our lives. He is the joy-giver.

## 6. Praise God with Thankful Hearts at All Times.

We read in Ephesians 5:19-20:

*Speak out to one another in psalms and hymns and spiritual songs, offering praise with voices [and instruments] and making melody with all your heart to the Lord.*

*At all times and for everything giving thanks in the name of our Lord Jesus Christ to God the Father.*

 According to Ephesians 5:19-20, when are we to give thanks to the Lord, and what are some valuable ways to give praise?

Voicing praise and thanks to the Lord brings encouragement to us. It is so important to our emotional and spiritual health. A negative situation can be turned completely around through praise and thanksgiving. Paul tells us in 1 Thessalonians 5:16-18:

*Be happy [in your faith] and rejoice and be glad-hearted continually (always);*

*Be unceasing in prayer [praying perseveringly];*

*Thank [God] in everything [no matter what the circumstances may be, be thankful and give thanks], for this is the will of God for you [who are] in Christ Jesus [the Revealer and Mediator of that will].*

**Question:** What are we instructed to do in these verses?

**Question:** Why are we to give thanks in everything?

**Question:** Have you focused on rejoicing and being glad-hearted and giving thanks no matter what the circumstance?

**Question:** If so, what have you experienced?

One day my husband called me while I was out shopping to tell me that he had lost his day-timer. He is a salesman, and he had all his appointments as well as other very important information in his day-timer. I told him that I would help him look for it when I returned home, but He told me that he knew it wasn't there.

In looking back, he remembered laying the day-timer on the trunk of his car. Before leaving to run an errand, he realized that the trash truck had come, and he decided to bring the trashcans into the garage. After retrieving the trashcans, he got into his car and forgot all about the day-timer.

At the time of his call to me, he was in his car backtracking where he had driven after leaving our home. I told him that I would pray. After I got off the phone with him, I began to thank God for His goodness. I had just read a book that talked about the power of thanksgiving. I asked God to help Pete find the day-timer, but mostly, I simply thanked God for His goodness and faithfulness.

Pete did not return home until late that night because he had a dinner meeting to attend that evening. We talked briefly the next morning. He had not found the day-timer. I told him we would continue to pray. I continued to thank God for His faithfulness. Later that morning, Pete called to tell me that a former coworker had phoned to tell him that she had his day-timer.

A man who was traveling on a busy road near our home had seen the day-timer on the road, and he stopped to pick it up. Pete's name was not in the day-timer, so he called one of the numbers he found in it. He called just the right person, and she told him that she knew exactly who the owner was. She called Pete, and he was able to pick it up later that day.

Even if the day-timer had not been found, I know that God would have been faithful to make a way to retrieve the information. Having it returned, however, was extremely exciting. It is so exciting to move into an attitude of praise and thanksgiving, and then watch God move on our behalf.

I have determined in my heart that I am going to give God thanks in all circumstances. God takes the difficulties in our lives, and He turns them around when we have thankful hearts. It is not difficult to give Him thanks because He is always faithful, no matter what.

*Experiencing God's Abundant Joy*

I have seen wonderful results from giving thanks time and time again. A joyful and thankful heart releases God's goodness into the situations of our lives.

*Lesson Application:* Take some time to thank God for His goodness and faithfulness in your life. Thank Him for the everlasting joy that comes to you through the redemptive work of the cross. Ask God to lead you to Scripture that will assist you in walking in the joy of the Lord. Ask Him to help you give thanks in all circumstances and to rejoice always. Begin to list the things for which you are thankful. Ask Jesus to let His streams of living water flow through your life continually.

*"Rejoice in the Lord always [delight, gladden yourselves in Him]; again I say, Rejoice! Let all men know and perceive and recognize your unselfishness (your considerateness, your forbearing spirit). The Lord is near [He is coming soon]."*
*Philippians 4:4-5*

*Dear Lord,*

*Thank You for Your amazing love and grace and goodness in my life. Help me to walk in the fullness of Your Spirit every day. I want to rejoice always. I want to walk in obedience and love moment-by-moment. Let Your joy overflow in my life, and make me a blessing everywhere I go. Help me be happy and glad-hearted continually. Help me to dwell in Your presence always. Thank You for giving me beauty instead of ashes and the oil of joy instead of mourning. Help me wear the garment of praise everywhere I go.*

*In Jesus' precious name,*

*Lesson Seven*

# EXPERIENCING GOD'S WONDERFUL PEACE

*"I will listen [with expectancy] to what God the Lord will say, for He will speak peace to His people..." Psalm 85:8*

**Lesson Focus:** When we put our trust in God's Word and His Spirit, we find deep and lasting peace.

**Introduction:** There is not a problem in this world that God cannot solve. He has an answer for every difficult situation we face in life. It is only when we take our eyes off the truths and promises of His Word that we lose our peace. As we place our trust in Jesus, His peace will guard our hearts and our minds, no matter how difficult the circumstances of our lives.

When Jesus is our Shepherd, He leads us beside still and restful waters. There is never any reason to fear or become anxious when Jesus is Lord of our lives because He is always with us. He provides protection, comfort, and guidance. He makes provision for us in the presence of our enemies. When Jesus is our Shepherd, His goodness, mercy, and unfailing love follow us everywhere we go (Psalm 23).

Jesus defeated our enemies at the cross, and He has given us authority to use His powerful name. When we dwell in His presence, He enables us to remain stable and secure in every situation. When we lean and rely on Him, He will always make a way for us. He will direct our steps and show us the right path to take (Proverbs 3:5-6). We never need to fear because He will give us His strength, help, and support. He will hold us up and preserve us with His power and might (Isaiah 41:10).

When we make the Lord our refuge, He protects us from evil. He sends His angels to guard and defend us. They watch over us and they support us in everything we do and everywhere we go. We have been given the awesome ability to trample upon our enemy. The Lord is our defender, and when we call on Him, He will answer us, deliver us, and honor us (Psalm 91).

When we make the Lord our refuge and our fortress, we will have perfect peace. Scripture tells us, *"A righteous man may have many troubles, but the Lord delivers him from them all"* (Psalm 34:19 NIV).

In our last lesson, it was stated that joy is the distinguishing mark of the victorious Christian life. Peace is another distinguishing mark of a victorious life. When we rest and trust in God's faithfulness, we will walk in peace. Jesus is our Prince of Peace, and when we abide in Him, we abide in His peace.

# SIX VALUABLE KEYS TO WALKING IN PEACE

## 1. Stay Your Mind on the Lord.

We read in Isaiah 26:3-4:

> *You will* guard him and *keep him in perfect* and *constant peace whose mind [both its inclination and its character] is stayed on You, because he commits himself to You, leans on You,* and *hopes confidently in You.*
>
> *So trust in the Lord (Commit yourself to Him, lean on Him, hope confidently in Him) forever; for the Lord God is an everlasting Rock [the Rock of Ages].*

 According to Isaiah 26:3, what does the Lord do for the person who stays his mind on Him?

 Why are we encouraged to put our trust in the Lord (v. 4)?

As I shared in lesson five, our son Michael went through a very difficult struggle with anxiety. There were many weapons of the Spirit that he learned to use during that time. One of the major weapons came from Isaiah 26:3. Often when we prayed, God would bring verses to mind that gave Michael insight into how to stand against the attacks.

One morning Michael came under an intense attack. As we

prayed, God brought Isaiah 26:3 to mind. It was clear that God wanted Michael to focus his thoughts on Him. I suggested that he go to his room and begin reading in Psalms or Proverbs. The Word is such a powerful way to stay our mind on the Lord. These two books are always a good place to turn to when we are anxious because there are amazing promises as well as awesome words of wisdom and instruction recorded in these books.

Michael received the counsel, and he went to his room to read. About 30 minutes later he came out of his room, and he told me the anxiety had lifted. He was very encouraged. I suggested that he write Scripture promises on index cards to keep with him, so that any time he came under an attack of anxiety, he could pull the cards out and begin to focus his thoughts on the Lord.

For several years, Michael carried these Scripture cards with him everywhere he went. I often asked him if he had his Scripture cards with him, and he would pat his pocket, indicating that the cards were in his pocket. During that time, he developed a tremendous love for the Word of God that remains to this day.

## 2. Stay Committed to the Word.

We read in Psalm 119:165:

*Great peace have they who love Your law; nothing shall offend them* or *make them stumble.*

Proverbs 3:1-2 tells us:

*My Son, forget not my law* or *teaching, but let your heart keep my commandments;*

*For length of days and years of a life [worth living] and tranquility [inward and outward and continuing through old age till death], these shall they add to you.*

 According to Psalm 119:165, what happens in the life of a person who loves God's Word?

 According to Proverbs 3:1-2, what happens to those who obey the Word of God?

The Word of God greatly improves our quality of life. Inward and outward peace come through the Word. It can even be felt in our homes. Since I began to give God's Word priority in my life, I have had many friends tell me that they can feel peace in my home. The more we stay in the Word, the more peace there will be in our lives and in our homes.

## 3. Live a Righteous Life—Yielded to the Holy Spirit.

We read in Isaiah 32:17-18:

> *The fruit of righteousness will be peace; the effect of righteousness will be quietness and confidence forever.*
>
> *My people will live in peaceful dwelling places, in secure homes, in undisturbed places of rest (NIV).*

 According to Isaiah 32:17-18, how do we receive peace?

Paul tells us in 2 Corinthians 5:21:

> *For our sake He made Christ [virtually] to be sin Who knew no sin, so that in and through Him we might become [endued with, viewed as being in, and examples of] the righteousness of God [what we ought to be, approved and acceptable and in right relationship with Him, by His goodness].*

**Question:** How does Paul tell us we are we made righteous in this verse?

**Question:** From the following verses in 2 Corinthians, how can we maintain peace?

- 2 Cor. 1:3-4—

- 2 Cor. 3:17—

- 2 Cor. 4:16-18—

- 2 Cor. 5:7—

- 2 Cor. 9:8—

- 2 Cor. 10:3-5—

Peace is the fruit of following the leadership of the Holy Spirit and the counsel of the Word. When we follow the Word of God, we will find peace. When we choose what is right, we will walk in peace. True peace comes when we walk by faith and not by sight (2 Cor. 5:7). If we reverse the order and start walking by sight, we will become discouraged. Walking by sight will cause us to lose our peace every time.

The enemy of our souls wants us to believe his lies. He wants us to keep us in turmoil in our thought lives. As we renew our minds to the Word, wrong patterns of thinking are exposed. As we stay focused on the Word, the truths we find will enable us to know and understand that *"all things are possible with God"* (Mark 10:27).

Why should we worry and fret when God is our everlasting Rock? He is in charge of the entire universe. He is Lord over all things, and He is completely trustworthy all the time. He has given us powerful spiritual weapons. As we place our trust in Him, He will enable us to bring every thought into obedience to the mind of Christ (2 Corinthians 10:5). When our thoughts line up with His, we will have perfect peace.

## 4. Pray with Thanksgiving About Everything.

Paul tells us in Philippians 4:6-7:

> *Do not fret or have any anxiety about anything, but in every circumstance and in everything, by prayer and petition (definite requests), with thanksgiving, continue to make your wants known to God.*
>
> *And God's peace [shall be yours, that tranquil state of a soul assured of its salvation through Christ, and so fearing nothing from God and being content with its earthly lot of whatever sort that is, that peace] which transcends all understanding shall garrison and mount guard over your hearts and minds in Christ Jesus.*

**Question:** According to Philippians 4:6-7, what are we instructed to do with anxiety?

**Question:** What are we told will happen when we go to God with prayer and thanksgiving?

**Question:** What difference has prayer with thanksgiving made in your life?

In Hannah Whitall Smith's book *The God Of All Comfort*, she writes:

> If we want to be comforted, we must make up our minds to believe every single solitary word of comfort God has ever spoken; and we must refuse utterly to listen to any words of discomfort spoken by our own hearts, or by our circumstances. We must set our faces like a flint to believe, under each and every sorrow and trial, in the divine comforter, and to accept and rejoice in His all-embracing comfort. I say, "set our faces like a flint," because, when everything around us seems out of sorts, it is not always easy to believe God's words of comfort. We must put our wills into this matter of being comforted, just as we have to put our wills into all other matters in our spiritual life. We must choose to be comforted.[1]

We must set our wills to walk in peace. We need to determine to rest and trust in God, no matter what. God is faithful and He is trustworthy. Therefore, we can be peaceful in the storms of life. God has promised us protection from the terrors of the night and the evil arrows of our enemy that come in the day. He has promised us protection from pestilence and plagues. When we make Him our refuge, He has promised us that no harm will come near our dwelling place (Psalm 91). He is completely faithful, and He is completely trustworthy.

## 5. Cast All Your Care on the Lord.

We are given clear instructions in 1 Peter 5:7 regarding peace. Peter tells us:

> *Casting the whole of your care [all your anxieties, all your worries, all your concerns, once and for all] on Him, for He cares for you affectionately and cares about you watchfully.*

 What does Peter instruct us to do in this verse, and why?

Trusting completely in the Lord is not always easy. Often we give all our concerns to Him, and then we take them back. When we struggle to cast all our care on the Lord, it is very helpful to ask faithful Christian friends and family members to pray and stand with us. Through the power of God's Word, along with the amazing power of prayer and godly counsel, God will move us into a place of peace and rest. He is always working for our good because He desires the very best for us.

## 6. Know that God is Working for Your Good.

Paul tells us in Romans 8:28:

> *And we know that all things work together for good to those who love God, to those who are the called according to His purpose.*

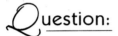 According to Romans 8:28, what can we be certain of when we walk through difficulties?

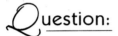 How have you seen God work difficult situations together for your good?

Time and time again, I have experienced God's faithfulness in the midst of intense trials. The summer that I first put these lessons together, I found myself in some very difficult situations.

My twin sister was struggling with severe depression, and I told her that I would come pick her up at her home in Tennessee. I wanted to encourage her. The next morning, while I was making my plans to go to my sister's, I received a call from my dad telling me that my mother was in the hospital. Dad had found mother passed out in the bathroom early that morning. After rushing her to the hospital, they discovered colon cancer. She was in surgery at the time of his call. I told my dad that I would come as soon as I could. My mom and dad lived a couple of hours away.

I called my sister to tell her that I would need to wait a while before I came to get her. I then drove to be with my mother at the hospital. When I arrived, my mom was out of surgery, and I was told that she was doing well. It was a wonderful answer to prayer. After my mother came out of recovery, one of her concerns was for my older brother. She had not been able to get in touch with him for several days. As it turned out, she was not able to reach him because he was in jail.

All of these circumstances could have overwhelmed me, but I was determined that I was not going to lose my victory or my peace. I made a decision that day that I was going to walk in victory, no matter what. I had been spending a great deal of time focusing on the Word, and I knew that God would be faithful.

There were some very significant things that God did during that time. I was able to pray the prayer of salvation with my dad. Dad was in church, but I was not certain of his salvation. Dad prayed the prayer with me, and we saw some wonderful changes in him. I picked up my sister, and she was able to help with mother's recovery. The time spent with mother was a blessing to her. I was able to pray with my brother and minister to him. We can have peace in the midst of the storms of life.

*Walking in Victory*

**Lesson Application:** Take some time to cast all your cares, burdens, and anxiety on the Lord. Take time to stay your mind on Him. Determine in your heart that you are going to rest in God's faithfulness, no matter what. Ask God to lead you to passages of Scripture that will give you peace. Ask Him to give you specific promises that will minister to your personal needs, and then spend time meditating on His promises.

*"And God is able to make all grace abound to you, so that in all things at all times, having all that you need, you will abound in every good work."*
*2 Corinthians 9:8 NIV*

*Dear Lord,*

*Please help me to believe Your words of comfort in every situation. Help me to stay my mind on You. Help me to refuse to listen to the lies of the enemy. Help me to walk in Your peace every day. I place my life in Your hands. Thank You that You are my Shepherd, and You lead me beside still and restful waters. Thank You for restoring my soul. Thank You for leading me and guiding me in Your peace. My prayer is for more of You—more of Your peace, more of Your grace, and more of Your presence in my life.*

*In Jesus' precious name,*

*Amen,*

## Notes

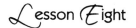

# GOD WILL GIVE YOU WISDOM

*"For the Lord gives skillful and godly Wisdom, and from His mouth come knowledge and understanding." Proverbs 2:6*

**Lesson Focus:** Through God's Word and through the revelation that the Holy Spirit gives, we will find all the wisdom, understanding, insight and knowledge we need to live victorious lives.

**Introduction:** God is faithful to lead and direct us in the big and small details of our lives. As we seek His wisdom, He will be faithful to give us scriptural principles and instructions to assist and guide us in every decision we make. When we rest and trust in Him, wisdom and insight will be revealed to us. As we treasure God's Word in our hearts, we will have the knowledge and understanding we need to live successful lives.

Scripture tells us, *"The fear of the Lord is the beginning of Wisdom; a good understanding have all those who do His commandments..."* (Psalm 111:10 NKJV). The Hebrew word for fear in this verse also means *reverence*.[1] It is so important for us to reverently fear the Lord through holding firmly to His instructions and counsel. We walk in godly wisdom through following God's Word and His Spirit.

It is foolish for us to think that we can accomplish anything of real value apart from God. When we need direction, it is extremely important to seek godly wisdom (James 1:5). God created the world and everything in it. He knows how it works and how it functions. He has knowledge and insight that no one else has. When we seek His counsel, He will give us clear direction, and He will show us what to do and what to say in every situation.

> IF WE WANT TO BE SECURE AND CONFIDENT IN OUR PLANS AND DECISIONS, IT IS ESSENTIAL THAT WE DO THINGS GOD'S WAY.

If we want to be secure and confident in our plans and decisions, it is essential that we do things God's way. Proverbs 1:33 tells us, *"But whoso hearkens to me [Wisdom] shall dwell securely and in confident trust and shall be quiet, without fear or dread of evil."* We discussed this verse in our lesson on obedience. When we obey God's instructions we are walking in wisdom, and through our obedience, we will be confident and secure. Jesus is the voice of wisdom, and as we listen to His voice, we will be able to confidently rest in His faithfulness.

God's Word is so amazing that even a single verse of Scripture can have a profound effect on us. There are times when all the insight we need can be found in one verse. As we set our hearts to diligently seek wisdom, we will find it. In this lesson, we are going to examine biblical principles that will assist and enable us to walk in godly wisdom every day of our lives.

# FIVE POWERFUL KEYS TO WALKING IN GODLY WISDOM

## 1. Reverently Fear and Worship the Lord.

In Psalm 111:10 the psalmist tells us:

> *The reverent fear and worship of the Lord is the beginning of Wisdom and skill [the preceding and the first essential, the prerequisite and the alphabet]; a good understanding, wisdom, and meaning have all those who do [the will of the Lord]. Their praise of Him endures forever.*

Question: According to Psalm 111:10, how do we gain wisdom and understanding?

Question: What happens when we are in the will of the Lord?

*Walking in Victory*

**Question:** In the following verses, what is promised to those who fear the Lord?

- Proverbs 10:27—

- Proverbs 14:26-27—

- Proverbs 19:23—

- Proverbs 22:4—

As we walk in reverential fear and worship of our Lord, we will receive wisdom that leads to life. Each time we experience the trustworthiness of God, our faith increases. As we walk in the wisdom that reverential fear brings, we can trust in God, knowing that He always has everything under control. Through the wisdom He provides, we can rest in His loving care without fear of harm. Through wisdom and sincere worship, a fortified place of refuge will be provided for us and for our children.

Contrast the difference between a man of wisdom and a man who ignores discipline in the following verses.

- Proverbs 10:17—

- Proverbs 10:23—

- Proverbs 13:15—

- Proverbs 13:18—

- Proverbs 15:32—

From these verses we can see how important it is to walk in godly wisdom. When we walk in reverential fear and sincere worship of our Lord, our desire will be to please Him.

A number of years ago, while on the phone with my longtime friend and prayer partner, Nancy, she spoke one word of wisdom that brought tremendous freedom to me. I was in a dilemma that day, and I asked Nancy to pray with me. While we were praying, she said, "I heard one word—control." I realized at that moment that God was telling me that I needed to let go of control in the situation that was causing my dilemma. I was trying to hold onto control, and therefore, I was not trusting God.

When the Lord pointed out my sin through my trusted friend, I asked her to pray that I would let go and trust God. Then I prayed and I confessed my sin of not placing my complete trust in God. I gave control of the situation to the Lord. After we got off the phone, an amazing presence of God's peace came over me. I knew that God was going to work everything out in His perfect timing.

Within weeks, God had given my husband and me clear direction as to what to do in that situation. Things worked out so much better than I expected. God had a much better plan than I did. As long as I tried to work things out according to my way of thinking, I was going to remain frustrated. God does all things well, and it is wisdom for us to receive and act on His counsel.

**GOD DOES ALL THINGS WELL, AND IT IS WISDOM FOR US TO RECEIVE AND ACT ON HIS COUNSEL.**

## 2. Recognize that God's Love for you is Perfect.

Genuine wisdom comes through the knowledge of God's perfect love. His love is the most powerful force in the universe, and therefore, it is extremely important for us to understand His love for us. We read in 1 John 4:16-18:

> And we know (understand, recognize, are conscious of, by observation and by experience) and believe (adhere to and put faith in and rely on) the love God cherishes for us. God is love, and he who dwells and continues in love dwells and continues in God, and God dwells and continues in him.
>
> In this [union and communion with Him] love is brought to completion and attains perfection with us, that we may have confidence for the day of judgment [with assurance and boldness to face Him], because as He is, so are we in this world.
>
> There is no fear in love [dread does not exist], but full-grown (complete, perfect) love turns fear out of doors and expels every trace of terror! For fear brings with it the thought of punishment, and [so] he who is afraid has not reached the full maturity of love [is not yet grown into love's complete perfection].

 What does John tell us about God's love in this passage?

When God's love is perfected in our lives, we will be unaffected by future failure, crises, disaster, etc. Understanding God's perfect love enables us to let go and trust Him. When we are resting and trusting in God's perfect love, fear is driven out of our lives. Fear is the opposite of faith. Therefore, when we walk in perfected love, we will walk in wisdom that moves mountains.

## 3. Walk in Humility.

Letting go and trusting God requires humility, which goes hand-in-hand with perfected love. We are given wonderful instructions regarding the relationship between wisdom and humility in the third chapter of James. James 3:13-17 says:

> *Who is there among you who is wise and intelligent? Then let him by his noble living show forth his [good] works with the [unobtrusive] humility [which is the proper attribute] of true wisdom.*
>
> *But if you have bitter jealousy (envy) and contention (rivalry, selfish ambition) in your hearts, do not pride yourselves on it and thus be in defiance of* and *false to the Truth.*
>
> *This [superficial] wisdom is not such as comes down from above, but is earthy, unspiritual (animal), even devilish (demoniacal).*
>
> *For wherever there is jealousy (envy) and contention (rivalry and selfish ambition), there will also be confusion (unrest, disharmony, rebellion) and all sorts of evil* and *vile practices.*
>
> *But wisdom from above is first of all pure (undefiled); then it is peace-loving, courteous (considerate, gentle). [It is willing to] yield to reason, full of compassion and good fruits; it is wholehearted* and *straightforward, impartial* and *unfeigned (free from doubts, wavering, and insincerity).*

**Question:** According to James 3:13, how do we display true wisdom?

**Question:** To what does James attribute superficial wisdom in verses 14 and 15?

**Question:** According to James 3:16, what happens when there is jealousy and contention?

**Question:** What are the attributes of true wisdom recorded in verse17?

When we have all of the wonderful attributes of true wisdom operating in our lives, we will truly be walking in God's will. The more time we spend meditating in God's Word, the more wisdom we will display in our lives.

When I spent two months reading through God's Word for healing of my emotions, I had very little understanding in the natural realm of what was taking place in my soul and spirit. God was doing a work that was beyond my human understanding. I came out of that time with healing, but I gained so much more. God was planting wisdom in my heart through His Word.

After spending concentrated time in the Word, I had a foundation of knowledge and understanding to draw from that I did not have prior to that time. As I have continued in God's Word, the foundation has grown stronger, and it has enabled me to remain stable and secure through trials and difficulties.

## 4. Meditate Continually on God's Word.

We find some amazing words of instruction and encouragement in Psalms 119:97-105 regarding the wisdom and understanding that God imparts to those who meditate on His Word:

> *Oh, how I love Your law! It is my meditation all the day.*
>
> *You, through Your commandments, make me wiser than my enemies, for [Your words] are ever before me.*
>
> *I have better understanding and deeper insight than all my teachers, because Your testimonies are my meditation.*
>
> *I understand more than the aged, because I keep Your precepts [hearing, receiving, loving, and obeying them].*
>
> *I have restrained my feet from every evil way, that I might keep Your word [hearing, receiving, loving, and obeying it].*

*I have not turned aside from Your ordinances, for You Yourself have taught me.*

*How sweet are Your words to my taste, sweeter than honey to my mouth!*

*Through Your precepts I get understanding; therefore I hate every false way.*

*Your word is a lamp to my feet and a light to my path.*

 What encouragement does the psalmist give us in Psalm 119:97-105 regarding the value of God's Word to gain wisdom, understanding and insight?

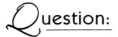 According to this passage, how does knowledge of God's Word protect us?

God's Word will give us all the wisdom we need for every situation. The Holy Spirit will direct us to passages of Scripture that will speak clearly to the circumstances of our lives. As we hear, receive, love, and obey the instructions of Scripture, we will gain insight and revelation that will make us wiser than our enemies. The Word of God is so powerful that it will give us deeper understanding than we can receive from all our teachers. It gloriously lights our way.

## 5. Treasure God's Word in Your Heart.

Solomon gives us outstanding instruction on wisdom in the book of Proverbs. Spending time in Proverbs is so valuable to us. Through the wisdom in this marvelous book, we will find healing, comfort, direction, freedom, and so much more. Let's take some time to examine the following words of instruction from Proverbs 2:1-8:

> *My Son, if you will receive my words and treasure up my commandment within you,*
>
> *Making your ear attentive to skillful* and *godly Wisdom* and *inclining and directing your heart* and *mind to understanding [applying all your powers to the quest for it];*
>
> *Yes, if you cry out for insight and raise your voice for understanding,*
>
> *If you seek [Wisdom] as for silver and search for skillful and godly Wisdom as for hidden treasure,*
>
> *Then you will understand the reverent* and *worshipful fear of the Lord and find the knowledge of [our omniscient] God.*
>
> *For the Lord gives skillful* and *godly Wisdom; from His mouth come knowledge and understanding.*
>
> *He hides away sound* and *godly Wisdom* and *stores it for the righteous (those who are upright and in right standing with Him); He is a shield to those who walk uprightly* and *in integrity,*
>
> *That He may guard the paths of justice; yes, He preserves the way of His saints.*

**Question:** In what ways are we encouraged to search for wisdom, understanding, and knowledge in Proverbs 2:1-8?

**Question:** According to this passage, if we diligently seek godly wisdom, what will God do for us?

**Question:** According to the following verses, what should we do if we discover that we are not operating in godly wisdom?

- 1 John 1:9—

- James 1:5—

- Colossians 3:16-17—

It is very exciting to know that God stores up godly wisdom for those who walk with Him. Through wisdom He guards and protects us. Through His Word He lights our way, and He gives us understanding and insight to know the right path to take. The more we yield to Wisdom—which is Jesus and His Word—the more we will experience the victorious Christian life.

R. A. Torrey writes in his book *Power-Filled Living:*

> There is more wisdom in the Bible than there is in all the other literature of the ages. The man who studies the Bible, even if he does not study any other book, will possess more real wisdom—wisdom that counts for eternity as well as time, wisdom that this perishing world needs, wisdom for which hungry hearts today are starving—than the man who reads every other book and neglects his Bible.[2]

*Lesson Application:* Ask God to help you walk in godly wisdom, understanding, insight, and knowledge every day. Determine that you will treasure His Word in your heart. Ask God to help you walk in reverential fear and worship of Him. Make a commitment that you are going to walk in humility and love. Make a conscious decision that you are not going to be guided by worldly counsel or worldly wisdom. Determine that you are going to walk in the wisdom that comes from above—wisdom that is pure and full of God's love.

*"The law of the Lord is perfect, reviving the soul. The statutes of the Lord are trustworthy, making wise the simple. The precepts of the Lord are right, giving joy to the heart. The commands of the Lord are radiant, giving light to the eyes. The fear of the Lord is pure, enduring forever. The ordinances of the Lord are sure and altogether righteous. They are more precious than gold, than much pure gold; they are sweeter than honey, than honey from the comb. By them is your servant warned; in keeping them there is great reward."*
*Psalm 19:7-11 NIV*

*Dear Lord,*

*Thank You for Your powerful Word that imparts such amazing wisdom and life to me. Thank You for helping me walk in godly wisdom and insight every day. It is only through Your Truth that I find freedom. I am so grateful for the wisdom and knowledge You impart to me from Your Word and Your Spirit. Open the eyes of my heart and give me deeper insight into the wonderful truths of Your Word. Help me to walk in humility and love. Help me to be pure, kind, courteous, and full of compassion and good works.*

*In Jesus' precious name,*
*Amen,*

*Lesson Nine*

# LIVING IN VICTORIOUS FAITH

*"Now faith is being sure of what we hope for and certain of what we do not see." Hebrews 11:1 NIV*

**Lesson Focus:** A wonderful life of victorious faith comes through believing and trusting in God's powerful Word and Holy Spirit presence. As we walk in love and obedience to God's Word and Spirit, we will accomplish great and mighty things.

**Introduction:** Faith is a powerful force. The Bible is full of faith-filled stories of all kinds of people who experienced amazing things because they believed in an all-powerful, Almighty God. Shadrach, Meshach and Abednego's faith saved them from the fiery furnace. Daniel's faith saved him from the mouth of the lions. David's faith conquered Goliath. Abraham's faith made him the father of many nations. Elijah and Elisha's faith raised the dead. The list goes on and on.

Jesus told us if we have faith the size of a mustard seed that nothing will be impossible for us (Matthew 17:20). He also said that our faith could move mountains (Matthew 21:21). This is extraordinary! As we trust in God's promises and His faithfulness, we will see mountains of adversity removed from our lives.

Jesus told us that if we would believe and not doubt we could have whatever we asked for in prayer (Mark 11:23-24). Then He told us in the next verse (Mark 11:25) to forgive when we pray. Love and forgiveness are essential to a life of faith. As we walk in the love of God, faith is activated because faith works by love (Galatians 5:6).

We read in Romans 10:17 that faith comes through hearing God's Word. As we have seen in previous lessons, obeying God's Word enables us to abide in His love (John 15:10). Love and obedience are indispensable to a life of faith. When we walk in faith that is motivated by love, we will see amazing answers to our prayers.

When we truly understand that God is love, and His Word is true, a wonderful door of faith opens to us. As we surrender to Jesus as our Savior and Lord, we begin our glorious walk of faith. Our goal is to live by faith in everything we do and everything we say. It is God's will and His design for us to live a life of exceptional faith. Walking by faith may not always be easy, but it is extremely rewarding. In this lesson, we are going to look at some valuable keys to walking and living in victorious faith.

# SEVEN VALUABLE KEYS TO LIVING IN VICTORIOUS FAITH

## 1. Know that God is Always Truthful.

We find an amazing declaration in Numbers 23:19 where the Scripture tells us:

*God is not a man, that He should lie, nor a son of man, that He should change His mind. Does He speak and then not act? Does he promise and not fulfill?*

 What does Numbers 23:19 tell us about the faithfulness and truthfulness of God?

 According to this verse, how dependable are the promises of God?

Throughout His earthly ministry, Jesus repeated over and over the phrase, *"Truly I tell you."* He told us that He is *"the Way and the Truth and the Life"* (John 14:6). The Father, Son, and Holy Spirit are completely trustworthy. Jesus' words—His truths—are spirit and life. We can completely depend on His Word to impart life to us in every situation (John 6:63). Through the power of God's Word and His Spirit, God will make a way for us, no matter what it looks like or how it appears in the natural realm.

We need to go before God's throne of grace to receive His guidance and direction. As we do, the Holy Spirit will lead us to promises in the Word that will speak into our circumstances. We can then take those promises and begin to meditate on them and hold firmly to them. Holding firmly to the promises of God will enable faith to arise in our hearts to see the fulfillment of all that God has promised. We can completely trust God to be totally faithful and true to His Word.

## 2. Recognize that Faith Comes by Hearing the Word.

We are told in Romans 10:17:

*So then faith comes by hearing, and hearing by the word of God (NKJV).*

 According to Romans 10:17, how important is hearing the Word of God?

 From the following verses, what are some valuable ways to hear God's Word?

- Joshua 1:8—

- Psalm 119:13-15—

- Psalm 119:52—

- Proverbs 10:8—

- Proverbs 13:2—

**uestion:** According to Revelation 12:11, what happens to our enemy when we give voice to the testimonies of God (His Word) along with personally testifying to His faithfulness?




A very powerful way to hear the Word of God is to speak it from our lips. We are told in Romans 10:17 that faith is imparted to us as we hear the Word. One of the main aspects of scriptural meditation is speaking the Word of God out of our mouths. As we proclaim the Word of God, it is planted in our hearts and in our minds. As we speak the Word, it is cultivated in the soil of our hearts, and our faith is energized and strengthened.

When we are discouraged, it is extremely helpful to read favorite passages of Scripture out loud. Through voicing the testimonies of God, we overcome our enemies. As we give voice to the Word, we are strengthened and encouraged. Our hearts and our minds are empowered as we hear words of Truth coming from our lips.

## 3. Recognize the Importance of Choosing Truth.

In the following verses, we receive valuable insight regarding the importance of choosing Truth:

> *I have chosen the way of truth* and *faithfulness; Your ordinances have I set before me. I cleave to Your testimonies... I will [not merely walk, but] run the way of Your commandments... (Psalm 119:30-32).*

> *And I will walk at liberty* and *at ease, for I have sought and inquired for [and desperately required] Your precepts (Psalm 119:45).*

***This is my comfort** and **consolation in my affliction; that Your word has revived me** and **given me life** (Psalm 119:50).*

**Question:** What did the palmist do in verses 30-32 of Psalm 119?

**Question:** According to Psalm 119:45 and 50, why is it important for us to follow the Truth of God's Word?

We need to determine in our hearts that God's Word is true. We need to make a conscious choice that we are going to believe God's Word no matter how we feel or what we see in the natural realm.

I mentioned in lesson one of this study that I met some wonderful ladies at a Bible Study when I was in my late twenties who taught me about the power of God's Word to impart life and health. I shared in that lesson my testimony of receiving emotional healing through the counsel of the Word and the Holy Spirit. Prior to my receiving emotional healing, I received a wonderful healing in my body. Through the healing in my body, a foundation of faith was laid that enabled me to believe God for emotional healing a number of years later.

Not long after I began attending the Bible Study that was so instructive and helpful, I began experiencing intense pain in my body. The medication that my doctor prescribed was not effective in alleviating the pain. I prayed and I asked others to pray for me. I was counseled to diligently search the Word of God for healing scriptures.

At that time, the Spirit of God made me aware that I was under attack. The intent of my enemy was to bring as much discouragement to me as possible, but God had a different plan. The more I meditated on healing scriptures, the more strength I received to walk in faith, and I began to walk free from the pain.

One morning, after I had been walking in faith and experiencing great victory for a number of weeks, I woke up in extreme pain. I remember saying to the Lord, "I thought I was healed." I heard Him say, "Are you going to believe how you feel, or are you going to believe My Word?" I said, "I'm going to believe Your Word." The pain completely lifted that morning, and I had an amazing day.

There were numerous times when the battle did not lift that quickly, and I would need to call friends for prayer. As they stood in agreement with me, I was always blessed. I continued to stand in faith, and there came a time when the battle was completely over. The battle did not end quickly. It took persistent faith, and there were times that the battle was very intense. As I pressed through to victory, I was able to build a foundation of faith that has helped me through many tests and trials.

Standing in faith in one battle strengthens us for the next battle we face. Every victory strengthens our faith for the next challenge. There may be times when we become very discouraged, but it is important to press on toward the goal to freedom and victory.

The battles I face today do not last as long as the battles I faced when I was first learning to walk by faith. As my faith has grown, and I have planted God's Word solidly in my heart, I have been able to recognize with greater ease the strategies of the enemy. As I have built a foundation of faith on the truthfulness of God's Word, I have been strengthened to face the storms of life.

## 4. Lay Your Foundation on The Rock.

Jesus asked a question in Luke 6:46, and then in verses 47-49, He tells how important it is to heed His words:

> *Why do you call Me, Lord, Lord, and do not [practice] what I tell you?*
>
> *For everyone who comes to Me and listens to My words [in order to heed their teaching] and does them, I will show you what he is like:*
>
> *He is like a man building a house, who dug and went down deep and laid a foundation upon the rock; and when a flood arose, the torrent broke against that house and could not shake or move it, because it had been securely built or founded on a rock.*
>
> *But he who merely hears and does not practice doing My words is like a man who built a house on the ground without a foundation, against which the torrent burst, and immediately it collapsed and fell, and the breaking and ruin of that house was great.*

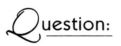

According to Jesus' instructions in the preceding verses, how do we develop unwavering, rock-solid faith?

**Question:** According to this passage, what happens to those who do not heed Jesus' words?

If we will purpose in our hearts to hear God's Word and do what it says, we will become mighty in faith. The storms of life will not overtake us when we remain faithful to the truths of Scripture. Through faith in God's Word, our lives will be built on a solid foundation—the Word of God and our immovable rock, Jesus Christ.

As we have seen, we are not asked to do anything in our own strength. We have a wonderful helper and friend in the Holy Spirit. As we lean on Him, He will lead us and guide us. He will strengthen and support us every step of the way.

## 5. Cultivate the Soil of Your Heart.

In Mark chapter 4, Jesus compares the Word of God to seed sown in an individual's heart. In verses 14-20 He tells us:

*The sower sows the Word.*

*The ones along the path are those who have the Word sown [in their hearts], but when they hear, Satan comes at once and [by force] takes away the message which is sown in them.*

*And in the same way the ones sown upon stony ground are those who, when they hear the Word, at once receive and accept and welcome it with joy;*

*And they have no real root in themselves, and so they endure for a little while; then when trouble or persecution arises on account of the Word, they immediately are offended (become displeased, indignant, resentful) and they stumble and fall away.*

*And the ones sown among the thorns are others who hear the Word;*

*Then the cares and anxieties of the world and distractions of the age, and the craving and passionate desire for other things creep in and choke and suffocate the Word, and it becomes fruitless.*

*And those sown on the good (well-adapted) soil are the ones who hear the Word and receive and accept and welcome it and bear fruit—some thirty times as much as was sown, some sixty times as much, and some [even] a hundred times as much.*

 What happens when the Word of God is sown in good soil?

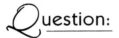 What happens when the seed of God's Word is sown in soil that is not well cultivated?

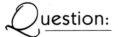 According to James 4:7-10, how can we guard against Satan stealing away the Word when it is sown in our hearts?

**Question:** According to Psalm 1:1-3 and John 15:4-5, how can we make our hearts good soil for the Word to prosper and grow?

It is so important for us not to become offended when circumstances arise in our lives that we do not understand. We need to remember that God is good. We have an enemy who wants us to believe that God is not good.

We learn in James chapter one that it is the trials in our lives that cause us to grow into maturity. Our enemy is the one who is testing us to see if we will continue to trust God. God knows that when we stand in faith through trials, we will develop perseverance, and we will grow into maturity. With each test, our faith is strengthened, and we grow stronger for the next test.

I have often heard people say that they do not regret the tremendous trials they have experienced because the trials have caused them to press into God. After they are on the other side of the trial, they can truly see the good that came out of it. Those who have walked in faith through difficult trials will testify that God has taught them many valuable things.

## 6. Recognize that Faith is the Assurance of Things not Seen.

A life of faith is based on what God has proclaimed in His Word. We can never base our faith on what we see or feel in the natural realm because we can only see and perceive to a small degree with our natural eyes and our natural senses. When we come into the kingdom of God, we have the privilege of accessing the kingdom realm, and the kingdom realm has no limits. What cannot be perceived in the natural can be accessed in the realm of the Spirit. Therefore, we are told in Hebrews 11:1:

> **Now faith is the assurance (the confirmation, the title deed) of the things [we] hope for, being the proof of things [we] do not see** *and the conviction of their reality [faith perceiving as real fact what is not revealed to the senses].*

**Question:** What can we learn from Hebrews 11:1 when we are holding to a promise of God that we cannot see with our eyes or perceive with our senses?

**Question:** According to Hebrews 11:6, how important is faith?

**Question:** What are we encouraged to do in the following verses when we cannot see the fullness of the promise of God?

- 2 Corinthians 5:7—

- Hebrews 10:35-36—

- Hebrews 10:38—

- Hebrews 12:1-3—

As we persevere in faith, trusting in the faithfulness of God's Word and trusting in the Holy Spirit for guidance, we will walk victoriously. We never need to fear or doubt the goodness or trustworthiness of God. It is so important that we throw off everything that hinders. Jesus came to give us abundant life (John 10:10). Therefore, in the midst of difficulties, it is important that we keep our eyes fixed on Jesus. He is our light and our salvation (Psalm 27:1). He brings comfort and protection in the most difficult times, and He gives hope for the future.

When I was struggling with intense physical pain, I was often awake in the middle of the night. One night I said, "God where are You?" I heard Him say, "I am right here with you." I immediately thought of Hebrews 13:5 where He tells us that He will never leave us or forsake us. God was with me, and He was supporting me the entire time. I was in a battle, but God was with me. He continually sent me help, through the Holy Spirit and through people who stood with me in prayer. As I continued to stand in faith, there came a day when the battle ended, and I was free.

It is so important to fix our eyes on Jesus. Through His Word and His Spirit, we will be strengthened and encouraged. When we are a new creation, everything that we are is founded on Christ Jesus. He is the living Word of God, and as we focus on Him, faith will arise in our hearts and in our souls.

## 7. While you are Waiting on the Promise, Exercise Patience.

God never wants us to become discouraged in our faith. His Word is completely trustworthy. We are told in Hebrews 6:12 **...imitate those who through faith and patience inherit the promises (NKJV)**. It is so important that we learn to exercise patience when we are holding to God's promises. Jesus encouraged us with the following words in Mark 4:26-29:

*And He said, The kingdom of God is like a man who scatters seed upon the ground.*

*And then continues sleeping and rising night and day while the seed sprouts and grows and increases—he knows not how.*

*The earth produces [acting] by itself—first the blade, then the ear, then the full grain in the ear.*

*But when the grain is ripe and permits, immediately he sends forth [the reapers] and puts in the sickle, because the harvest stands ready.*

 As we compare the seed in this parable to the seed of God's Word, how does God's Word grow in our lives

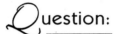 What do we need to do between the time we plant the Word in our hearts and the time of the fulfillment of the promise (Hebrews 6:12; Mark 4:26-29)?

Patience is an aspect of the fruit of the Spirit. As we yield to the Holy Spirit, He will help us walk in faith and patience while we are waiting on the promise of God. A.W. Tozer tells us in *The Pursuit Of God*:

> We must have faith, and let us not apologize for it, for faith is an organ of knowledge and can tell us more about ultimate reality than all the findings of science. We are not opposed

to science, but we recognize its proper limitations and refuse to stop where it is compelled to stop. The Bible tells of another world too fine for the instruments of scientific research to discover. By faith we engage that world and make it ours. It is accessible to us through the blood of the everlasting covenant. If we will believe we may even now enjoy the presence of God and the ministry of His heavenly messengers. Only unbelief can rob us of this royal privilege.[1]

The more we rest and trust in the faithfulness of God, the more we experience ultimate reality, which is God Himself. God's reality is the one in which we have the privilege of walking. We engage the kingdom of God and His righteousness through faith. Our God is a righteous God who is faithful to His Word. We can trust fully and completely in His promises and His faithfulness. We have the royal privilege of walking in all that He has promised us in His Word.

*L*esson *A*pplication: Take some time to make a personal commitment to the Lord to walk by faith and not by sight. Determine in your heart that you are going to keep your eyes fixed on Jesus and the wonderful promises of His Word. Determine that you are going to believe that the seed of God's Word is growing even when you cannot see it. Resolve in your heart to walk by faith every day, no mater what.

*"Though the fig tree does not blossom and there is no fruit on the vines, [though] the product of the olive fails and the fields yield no food, though the flock is cut off from the fold and there are no cattle in the stalls, yet I will rejoice in the Lord; I will exult in the [victorious] God of my salvation! The Lord God is my Strength, my personal bravery, and my invincible army; He makes my feet like hinds' feet and will make me to walk [not to stand still in terror, but to walk] and make [spiritual] progress upon my high places [of trouble, suffering, or responsibility]!"*
*Habakkuk 3:17-19*

*Dear Lord,*

*Thank You for Your incredible faithfulness to me. Thank You for making my feet like hind's feet so that I can make spiritual progress on the high places. Thank You for strengthening my faith daily in Your Word. I am so grateful for the royal privilege of enjoying Your wonderful presence in my life. The cry of my heart is, "More, Lord, more, more of Your love, more of Your grace, and more of Your presence in my life." Open my eyes to see wonderful and amazing things in Your Word!*

*In Jesus' precious name,*

*Amen*

# Notes

*Lesson Ten*

# RECOGNIZING WHO YOU ARE IN CHRIST

*"I have been crucified with Christ and I no longer live, but Christ lives in me. The life I now live in the body, I live by faith in the Son of God, who loved me and gave Himself for me." Galatians 2:20 NIV*

*Lesson Focus:* In this lesson, we will examine some remarkable scriptural truths regarding who we are in Christ.

*Introduction:* All who have committed their lives to Jesus are called to be His representatives. When we live victorious lives, we represent Jesus well. Jesus walked in victory every day, and it is His sincere desire that we walk in victory as well. The crucifixion did not appear to be a day of victory, but victorious days are often disguised. What looked like a tremendous defeat became the most amazing victory that the world has ever known. As believers, we have the wonderful privilege to share in Jesus' awesome triumph at the cross.

When we accept Jesus as our Savior and Lord, we become a new creation. Our old life has passed away, and we have been made new (2 Cor. 5:17). We have been crucified with Christ, and we now live by faith (Gal. 2:20). Throughout the New Testament, we find amazing and powerful promises and statements regarding our position in the kingdom of God.

Our faithful Savior has given us everything we need to represent Him well. The more we comprehend and understand the magnificent truths of who we are in Christ, the more equipped we will be to walk in the fullness of our calling and fulfill our purpose in His kingdom.

As we review God's promises regarding who we are in Christ, it is important for us to remember that they are true whether we feel like they are true or not. When we are in Christ, we live by faith (2 Cor. 5:7). We have become one with our Savior, and He will enable us to accomplish everything that His Word says we can accomplish.

In Romans 4:17, the Scripture tells us, *"... God ... gives life to the dead and calls things that are not as though they were"* (NIV). We may not feel like we are who God says we are, but God's Word is true regardless of our feelings. Jesus has given believers the ability to do the same things that He did while He walked this earth (John 14:12-14). He has given us His power, authority, and ability (Luke 10:19). These are the statements and promises of Scripture, and *"God is not a man that He should lie, ..."* (Numbers 23:19).

We need to determine in our hearts that we are going to believe what God says about us no matter how we feel. We need to determine that we are going to walk by faith and not by sight in every situation. As we declare and decree God's Word over our lives, we will be strengthened and empowered to accomplish the things that He has called us to accomplish as co-heirs and co-laborers in His kingdom.

# TWELVE POWERFUL TRUTHS REGARDING WHO YOU ARE IN CHRIST

## 1. You Are the Salt of the Earth and the Light of the World.

We read in Matthew 5:13-14:

*You are the salt of the earth...You are the light of the world. A city set on a hill cannot be hidden.*

Salt enhances the flavor of food and light enhances vision. Salt is used as a preservative, and both salt and light have healing benefits. In poetry, salt often refers to people of great kindness, reliability, and honesty. Salt and light are symbolic of those who bring God's goodness, kindness and grace to the world around them.

Our world desperately needs to taste and see that God is good. There is a tremendous need for God's grace and kindness to be expressed to the world. We are the ones God has chosen to be salt and light. When we walk in the abundant grace and love of our Savior, people will be able to taste and see the good things of the kingdom of God. Do you see yourself as one who enables others to taste and see that God is good?

 What instruction and encouragement are we given in Isaiah 60:1-2, and what are the results in verse 3?

 **Question:** What do the following verses reveal to us regarding the power of the Word to impart life and light?

- Psalm 119:103-105—

- Psalm 119:130—

- Proverbs 6:23—

 **Question:** What are we told in John 1:1-5 and 14 about the source of this wonderful life and light?

When we commit our lives to Jesus, He imparts His amazing life to us, and He empowers us with the awesome privilege of bringing the life and light of God to those who are hurting and in need. Because we are salt and light, everywhere we go we bring the wonderful essence of God into the atmosphere around us. Through Jesus we bring light into the darkness.

## 2. All who are in Christ Have Authority Over the Enemy.

Jesus told us in Luke 10:19:

> *Behold! I have given you authority and power to trample upon serpents and scorpions, and [physical and mental strength and ability] over all the power that the enemy [possesses]; and nothing shall in any way harm you.*

 **Question:** What does Jesus promise us in Luke 10:19, and how does this promise strengthen your faith?

Jesus has given us power and authority over all the power of our enemy. This authority provides us with all the strength, ability, and protection we need to live triumphant lives. Everywhere we go, we carry the authority of God. This is truly amazing!

## 3. You Have Authority to use the Name of Jesus.

In John 14:12-14 Jesus tells us:

> *I assure you, most solemnly I tell you, if anyone steadfastly believes in Me, he will himself be able to do the things that I do; and he will do even greater things than these, because I go to the Father.*
>
> *And I will do [I Myself will grant] whatever you ask in My Name [as presenting all that I AM], so that the Father may be glorified and extolled in (through) the Son.*
>
> *[Yes] I will grant [I Myself will do for you] whatever you shall ask in My Name [as presenting all that I AM].*

 **Question:** What did Jesus promise those who believed in Him in the preceding verses?

: As you consider the fact that you have been given such amazing authority to use the name of Jesus, what should your response be to this wonderful call on your life?

We are promised something in the preceding verses that would be unbelievable if it had not come from the lips of Jesus. We have not only been given authority over our enemy, we have been given authority to do the same things that Jesus did. Jesus told us that we would do even greater things. This is absolutely remarkable!

## 4. You Are Jesus' Friend.

In John 15:15 Jesus says:

*I do not call you servants (slaves) any longer, for the servant does not know what his master is doing (working out). But I have called you My friends, because I have made known to you everything that I have heard from My father. [I have revealed to you everything that I have learned from Him].*

: According to John 15:15, how is a servant different from a friend?

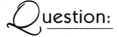: What should your response be to this amazing friendship?

To know that we are God's friends is very exciting because friends bless friends. While writing in my journal one day, I heard the Lord say, "Did you know that you are my friend?" Then I heard Him say, "Abraham was my friend, and Moses was my friend. You are no different." Jesus has called us His friends. The more our hearts seek and long after God, and the more we will understand His wonderful friendship, the more we will walk in the fullness of all the He has provided for us.

## 5. You Are One with Jesus, and You Have His Glory and Honor.

In John 17:21-22 Jesus prays:

*That they all may be one, [just] as You, Father, are in Me and I in You, that they also may be one in Us, so that the world may believe and be convinced that You have sent Me.*

*I have given to them the glory and honor which You have given Me, that they may be one [even] as We are one.*

 According to John 17:21-22, why have we been given the same glory and honor that the Father has given to Jesus, and why is this important?

 What does Psalm 133:1-3 reveal to us regarding the importance and value of unity?

We can never question our value in the kingdom when we come to truly understand Jesus' remarkable statements in John 17:21-22. It is important for us to spend time meditating on these powerful truths. God's anointing and blessing are released through our oneness in Christ. Jesus has given us His glory and honor, and this glorious privilege releases His anointing and blessing on our lives. As we walk in Jesus' glory and honor, we will accomplish extraordinary things.

We are Jesus' representatives, and it is His desire that the world see Him through us. When Jesus comes to dwell in us, we receive all that He is, and He is glorious and honorable. We cannot become one with Him without receiving all that He is. This is such an amazing privilege. There are no words to adequately describe this special place of honor in Him.

When we come to fully accept Jesus' powerful statements regarding our position in Him, nothing will be impossible for us because nothing is impossible for Him. Because we are one with Christ, all things are possible for us. To learn that He has given His glory and honor to us is astounding. Even though we do not deserve this amazing blessing, it is ours in Christ.

> **BECAUSE WE ARE ONE WITH CHRIST, ALL THINGS ARE POSSIBLE FOR US.**

## 6. The Father Loves You as He Loves Jesus.

Jesus prays these amazing words in John 17:23:

> *I in them and You in Me, in order that they may become* **one** *and perfectly united, that the world may know* *and [definitely] recognize that You sent Me and that You have loved them [even] as You have loved Me.*

 **Question:** What did Jesus tell us about the Father's love in John 17:23?

 **Question:** What do we learn about the Father's love from John 3:16-17?

The Father loves you with a love that is beyond measure. He longs to see you succeed in everything you do. His desire is for you to walk in the fullness of His love every day. As you do, others will come to know this same powerful love. You carry His love with you everywhere you go because He lives in you. Therefore, expect His love to minister to you and through you in everything you do.

## 7. You Are God's Child and a Joint Heir with Christ, and Therefore, You Have Become a King and a Priest.

We read in Romans 8:16-17:

> *The Spirit Himself [thus] testifies together with our own spirit, [assuring us] that we are children of God.*
>
> *And if we are [His] children, then we are [His] heirs also; heirs of God and fellow heirs with Christ....*

John tells us in Revelation 1:5-6:

> *...To Him who loved us and washed us from our sins in His own blood, and has made us kings and priests*

> to His God and Father, to Him be glory and dominion forever and ever. Amen (NKJV).

**Question:** What does Romans 8:16-17 and Revelation 1:5-6 reveal to us regarding our position in the kingdom of God?

**Question:** Because of our position in the kingdom, what can we expect from our Father?

There are secret service agents that surround us because of our position in the kingdom. These unseen angels are there to assist and protect. In the same way that earthly kings are provided with protection and assistance, God provides protection and assistance to those who have been adopted into His royal family.

When you consider the fact that you are God's child, and you are a joint heir with Christ, it should change the way you look at everything in life. You have become a co-heir with the King of Kings and the Lord of Lords, and He has made you a king and a priest. This is truly a position of authority and honor.

## 8. You Are More Than a Conqueror.

We are told in Romans 8:37:

> *Yet amid all these things we are more than conquerors and gain a surpassing victory through Him Who loved us.*

Paul shares some very remarkable things in Romans chapter 8. He asks the question in verse 31, *"If God is for us, who [can be] against us?"* He goes on to make some amazing statements about God's faithfulness and love in the closing verses of the chapter. He tells us that nothing in all of creation will ever be able to separate us from the love of God.

 How should the knowledge that we have been made more than conquerors combined with the revelation that nothing can separate us from God's love change the way we approach life?

Not long ago I found myself struggling with the feeling that I did not have favor with someone with whom I felt that favor was important. One afternoon, while praying about the situation, the Lord brought to mind the words of a song that expressed His amazing love for me. Then I heard Him say, "I love you." I sensed in my spirit that He was saying, "I love you, and that is what truly matters."

At that moment, the struggle completely lifted. Being reminded of God's love brings courage. My discouragement was conquered through the revelation of God's love. I later discovered that I had favor with this individual the whole time. God grants favor to those He loves, and He will give us all the favor we need to accomplish His purpose for our lives. He has made us more than conquerors.

## 9. You Are a New Creation.

Paul tells us in 2 Corinthians 5:17:

> *Therefore if any person is [engrafted] in Christ (the Messiah) he is a new creation (a new creature altogether); the old [previous moral and spiritual condition] has passed away. Behold, the fresh and new has come!*

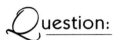 According to 2 Corinthians 5:17, what happens when we are engrafted in Christ, and why is this important?

It is so important for us to understand that our human spirit, our core being, is a new creation. The emotional struggles we face come from our soul—our mind, will, and emotions—not our born-again spirit. The more we renew our minds, the more our thoughts will come into agreement with our spirit man, which has been made new. As we renew our mind, bringing our soul into agreement with our born-again spirit, we will soar in God's kingdom.

## 10. You Are the Righteousness of God.

We read in 2 Corinthians 5:21:

> *For our sake He made Christ [virtually] to be sin Who knew no sin, so that in and through Him we might become [endued with, viewed as being in, and examples of] the righteousness of God [what we ought to be, approved and acceptable and in right relationship with Him, by His goodness].*

 What do we learn from 2 Corinthians 5:21 about who we are in Christ?

We have been made righteous because of the redeeming work of the cross. When we are in Christ, we are righteous because He is righteous. In the old covenant, when a sinner brought a lamb to be sacrificed for forgiveness of sin, the sinner was not examined, only the lamb. Our righteousness comes to us because Jesus is the spotless Lamb of God. We are not the ones who are examined. Jesus has been examined, and there is no imperfection in Him.

## 11. You Are Blessed with Every Spiritual Blessing in Christ.

Paul makes this powerful statement in Ephesians 1:3:

*May blessing (praise, laudation and eulogy) be to the God and Father of our Lord Jesus Christ (the Messiah) Who has blessed us in Christ with every spiritual (given by the Holy Spirit) blessing in the heavenly realm!*

 How have the gifts of the Spirit (Rom. 12: 6-8; 1 Cor. 12:7-11; and Eph. 4:11-13) and the fruit of the Spirit (Gal. 5:22-23) blessed your life?

 **Question:** How have you been blessed by the spiritual weapons (the Word, the name, the blood, etc.) and the spiritual armor (Eph. 6:10-17) that have been imparted to you by the Holy Spirit?

 **Question:** What does John tell us about the anointing of the Spirit (1 John 2:20, 27) and the power of prayer (1 John 5:14-15)?

We have been given everything we need to live victoriously. As we spend time in the Word, and we listen carefully to the Holy Spirit, we will find all the answers and help we need. There is nothing that we cannot accomplish in Christ. He has provided us with every spiritual blessing in the heavenly realm.

## 12. You Have Been Forgiven and Rescued From the Dominion of Darkness.

Paul tells us in Colossians 1:13-14:

> *[The Father] has delivered and drawn us to Himself out of the control and dominion of darkness and has transferred us into the kingdom of the Son of His love.*
>
> *In Whom we have our redemption through His blood, [which means] the forgiveness of our sins.*

*Recognizing Who You Are In Christ*

**Question:** Since we have been delivered out of the dominion of darkness, does our enemy have any authority or power over our lives?

**Question:** Have you fully received the forgiveness that Jesus purchased for you with His blood, or do you still carry guilt?

**Question:** How can the truths shared in this lesson enable you to walk free from guilt and shame?

**Question:** How can the truths in this lesson enable you to walk victoriously?

When we have been redeemed through the blood of Jesus, it is important for us to know and understand that our sins have been completely forgiven. It is very important that we understand that we are no longer under the authority of darkness. Sin no longer has any hold or power over us.

Jesus has delivered us from darkness, and the only power that Satan has is through deception. Therefore, his tactic is to use lies to control and discourage us. The goal of our enemy is always to kill, steal, and destroy (John 10:10). We need to stay on guard against Satan's lies. Every time we come out of agreement with a lie of the enemy, our enemy loses his hold in that area of our life.

A genuine revelation of the truth that we are completely forgiven and rescued from darkness is so freeing. Understanding who we are in Christ is very exciting. Through the revelation of the Word and the revelation of the Spirit, we have the ability to walk in complete freedom and victory!

*Lesson Application:* Spend time meditating on the scriptural truths recorded in this lesson. Let them sink deep into your heart. Focus on the fact that you are loved, you are righteous, and you are free from the dominion of darkness. Recognize that you are God's friend, and He loves to bless His friends. Begin to believe with all your heart that God's fullness dwells in you. Because of His fullness, you have the victory. Determine in your heart that you are not going to walk by sight. Determine that you are going to walk in the Truth of God's Word, no matter what.

Begin to confess what the Word says about you:

*"I am salt and light. I have authority over the enemy, and I have authority to use Jesus' name. I am God's child. He has made me a king and a priest, and therefore, I am more than a conqueror. I am God's friend. I am in Christ and I have His glory. I am a new creation and I am loved. I am the righteousness of God, and I am blessed with every spiritual blessing in Christ. I have been rescued from the dominion of darkness, and I have fullness of life in Christ!"*

*"For in Him the whole fullness of Deity (the Godhead) continues to dwell in bodily form [giving complete expression of the divine nature].*
*And you are in Him, made full and having come to fullness of life [in Christ you too are filled with the God-head—Father, Son, and Holy Spirit—and reach full spiritual stature]. And He is the Head of all rule and authority [or every angelic principality and power]."*
*Colossians 2:9-10*

*Dear Lord,*

*Thank You for making me more than a conqueror. I am so thankful for Your amazing love. Thank You that You have blessed me with every spiritual blessing in Christ, and thank You that I am seated in heavenly places with You. It is wonderful to know that I have been rescued from the dominion of darkness to walk in fullness of life. Thank You for making me salt and light. I commit myself completely to You. It is my sincere desire to represent You well! The cry of my heart is for more of You—more of Your love, more of Your grace, and more of Your presence in my life!*

*In Jesus' precious name,*

# Endnotes

## Lesson One
1. Andrew Murray, *The Best of Andrew Murray* (Grand Rapids, Michigan: Baker Book House, 1994), p. 46.

## Lesson Two
1. A. W. Tozer, Compiled by Edythe Draper, *The Pursuit Of God* (Camp Hill, PA: Christian Publications, Inc., 1995), p. 151.
2. James Strong, *Strong's Exhaustive Concordance Of The Bible* (Nashville: Crusade Bible Publishers, Inc.), Hebrew and Chaldee Dictionary, (1897), p. 32.
3. W. E. Vine, Merrill Unger, William White Jr., *Vines Complete Expository Dictionary Of Old And New Testament Words* (Nashville: Thomas Nelson Inc, Publishers, 1984), p. 400.

## Lesson Three
1. *Strong's*, Greek Dictionary of the N.T., (3306), p. 47.
2. Charles Spurgeon, *Joy In Christ's Presence* (New Kensington, PA: Whitaker House, 1997), pp. 72-73.

## Lesson Five
1. Microsoft Office: mac dictionary, 2008

## Lesson Seven
1. Hannah Whitall Smith, *The God Of All Comfort* (Chicago: Moody Press, 1956), p. 45.

## Lesson Eight
1. *Strong's*, Hebrew and Chaldee Dictionary (3374), p. 52.
2. R. A. Torrey, *Power-Filled Living* (New Kensington, PA: Whitaker House, 1998), p. 21.

## Lesson Nine
1. Tozer, *The Pursuit Of God*, p. 79.

# ABOUT THE AUTHOR

 has been leading and teaching Bible studies and prayer groups since 1979. She has been privileged to lead in women's ministry in various churches across the country. She began writing Bible study material in 1996 for the Women's Bible Study Ministry at her church in Colleyville, Texas. In 2002, God led Gaye and her husband to Gateway Church in Southlake, Texas, where she has served as a Women's Group Leader, Section Leader, and on the Women's Writing Team.

It is Gaye's sincere desire to see people living victorious lives. She serves as a spiritual mentor and mom to many. Her counsel and words of encouragement have blessed men, women, and children alike. God has used Gaye to bring hope and encouragement to women's groups, conferences, and retreats. It is the longing of her heart to see lives set free and transformed through God's Word and His Spirit. It is her heartfelt desire to see people walking in their divine destiny.

Gaye met her husband Pete while attending Midwestern State University. They married in January of 1970. Gaye's husband, children, and grandchildren are the joy and delight of her life.

Her husband is her strong supporter and counselor. Gaye's son has a master's degree in biblical studies from Regent College in Vancouver, British Columbia. Her daughter is a strong woman of faith who is raising her children to know the amazing love and grace of God. Her son-in-law is a graduate of Southwestern Theological Seminary in Fort Worth, Texas, and he serves as a minister in the Fort Worth area. God has used the testimonies from Gaye's family to confirm the power of His Word and Spirit time and time again.

Bringing hope and encouragement to the body of Christ has been the focus of Gaye's life and ministry. Because of the freedom that God has brought to her own life, Gaye has experienced firsthand the awesome declaration of Jesus, when He told His followers that He came to set the captives free (Luke 4:18). It is the longing of her heart to see people walking in genuine freedom and victory.

www.GayeMoss.com